ECCENTRIC MARKETING

ECCENTRIC MARKETING

Awakening the Arab Business World to the Benefits of Branding

SAID AGHIL BAAGHIL
ENTREPRENEUR, AUTHOR, SPEAKER,
AND MIND BEHIND ECCENTRIC MARKETING

EDITOR LESLIE WILHELM

iUniverse, Inc.
New York Lincoln Shanghai

Eccentric Marketing
Awakening the Arab Business World to the Benefits of Branding

iUniverse books may be ordered through booksellers or by contacting:

iUniverse
2021 Pine Lake Road, Suite 100
Lincoln, NE 68512
www.iuniverse.com
1-800-Authors (1-800-288-4677)

Because of the dynamic nature of the Internet, any Web addresses or links contained in this book may have changed since publication and may no longer be valid.

The views expressed in this work are solely those of the author and do not necessarily reflect the views of the publisher, and the publisher hereby disclaims any responsibility for them.

Cover Photography by Ghada Bakalla

ISBN: 978-0-595-46593-4 (pbk)
ISBN: 978-0-595-70358-6 (cloth)
ISBN: 978-0-595-90890-5 (ebk)

Printed in the United States of America

I am dedicating this book to My late grand father Abdallah Baaghil, My father Aghil Baaghil, to my beloved son Rakan Baaghil and to my life time best friend Munib Jawad

CONTENTS

ACKNOWLEDGEMENT

Ms. Siobhan Adams, the editor of *Gulf Marketing Review*, has been my true inspiration. She encouraged me to pursue the idea of writing this book. My opinions on regional changes in how companies in the Middle East perceive marketing had a monthly forum in *Gulf Marketing Review* until the very day that, with her encouragement, I started writing this book. I take this opportunity to thank Ms. Adams for her incredible support.

FOREWORD

By Jun Michael C. Dela Cruz, director of planning, LOGIC

Mr. Said Aghil Baaghil's type of eccentric marketing raises the eyebrows of many. For those who are new in this field, especially here in the Arab world, you might actually be shocked by the concepts introduced in this book. But truly, Eccentric Marketing has proven to click with Middle Eastern consumers based on what we have experienced in our company, LOGIC Brand Holdings. Baaghil's type of marketing targets human weakness and focuses on the pre-existing psychological choices of the human mind, which depend on different factors, such as age, upbringing, education, and more. By infusing his products with emotional attributes, he compels the target audience to patronize our products and services.

Many brands are so focused that they are working together to complete the circle of human needs. Baaghil's system of marketing has transformed failed companies and their products into winning brands. We have witnessed this in our former company, which eccentric marketing transformed.

Simultaneously managing his created brands, Baaghil has integrated marketing (in all its senses) and management, while experiencing both the strengths and weaknesses of each discipline. This enables him to specifically define and authoritatively discuss the current Middle Eastern situation, and present valid and commanding solutions to existing concerns. Baaghil and this book will show how companies can be transformed, influenced, and successful with Eccentric Marketing.

To benefit from reading his book requires two things: 1) have an open mind to understand and accept the situations and assessments presented, and 2) be ready to put into action the solutions or suggestions discussed, so that a positive output may be achieved. Unless these two things are met, consider your purchase of this book money thrown to waste.

Lastly, one can never be jack of all trades and one should not try. If you realizing that *focus* is required to make your company win, it is wise to turn to the advice of an Eccentric Marketing strategist. The choice is yours-…

ADDITIONAL ENDORSEMENTS:

"Said is a treasure in a sea of tired boring, repetitive ideas. Every interaction with him is a learning experience; I can confidently say he is a pioneer in marketing and many other fields. His understanding and grasp on the Western and the Middle Eastern cultures enable him to bring innovative and successful ideas to every concept".

—Anoir Adra—General Manager KSA Landmark PR & Events

"Mr. Said Baaghil's knowledge and creativity in marketing and brand creation is second to none. Anyone who has spoken with him even for only a few minutes can detect his true love of marketing and his energy for perfection which has proven to be a driving force apparent in his successful launch of Ventures in both the Western and Gulf markets."

—Sarah Abdullah, *Arab News* Business Journalist

INTRODUCTION

Why it is so important for our own brands to flourish in the global market, not just in the Middle East? Do CEOs or businesses owners in our region understand the importance of building brands? Some do, but most do not. Whether it's a small-scale or large-scale firm, most avoid the foreign language barrier and are comfortable only with the widely-spoken Arabic language. Thus, they promote their brands only within our region. This book, my first, will explore these and other issues and proposes a model for changing the region's approach to marketing, branding and ultimately selling products.

Today, the short- and long-term strategy that a firm adopts to sell its products and services depends on the firm's owner. He decides the fate of the brand—even if he is not knowledgeable about how to effectively apply basic marketing principles. Unfortunately, his ego does not serve him well when he makes critical decisions about the life-cycle of the brand and without even acknowledging the existence of the marketing department. One of the first points that an owner must consider, therefore, is this: As long as he works for the firm that he owns, he must act as an employee and must truly understand his job responsibilities before assigning himself the prestigious title of CEO.

Will things change?

As a result of these obstacles—our traditional business models and the egotistical CEO who doesn't understand marketing—the question that we face in the Middle East region every day is this: Will things change? Will firms work harder to transform themselves from established hierarchies to successfully cooperating team members? Growth cannot be properly measured when an establishment uses its resources in the wrong ways. Will the CEO or the owner admit his shortcomings and decide to do better for the region, his company and himself? I hope so, as we are all willing to push for progress.

Something must be changed, before our region awakens to the total losses it will face if we don't begin to marketing our products differently. In my opinion, if these changes don't take place now, we will continue to have cumulative, endless problems. As a marketing strategist who works with models that have attained positive results, I profess the importance of marketing with every business owner I meet. I tell them that marketing is the vital organ of their businesses; without it their doors will soon close.

Can we push for progress?

In this book, I also propose a solution to the business issues our region face. I call my technique "eccentric marketing," which is explained in detail, along with case studies showing proven results. I have developed hands-on applications that prove how effective the models of eccentric marketing are and will share them with you in this book.

Eccentric marketing adds value to the many great marketing applications available. The basic principle of eccentric marketing is the "fine touch," which focuses your product on specific demographic and psychographic characteristics of your target audience. This is done by identifying the needs of the audience and how those needs can be met. The process involves understanding the decisions your consumer makes (his mind), the perceptions he has of your product (his eyes) and the emotional bond he ultimately makes with your brand (his heart). These are the cornerstones of eccentric marketing and will be explained in detail in Chapter 4.

Eccentric marketing also presents a hands-on approach to marketing, rather than through static reports. Some consultants may provide you with sixty pages of documents full of facts, but without advice and analysis, you don't know if those facts will benefit your company or not.

Recently, I have pioneered eccentric marketing models in Jeddah, Saudi Arabia. I formed a company, named LOGIC, a for local business owner. It is a pure marketing firm that develops ideas into marketable brands. So far, the results have been outstanding, as you will see through some of the case studies we share in this book. LOGIC has established brands that are directly associated with the life style of the target audience and focused on their needs. The great part is that the consumer—the targeted audience—has bonded to the brand we have launched in a way that has created an emotional love between the brand and consumer. For example, LOGIC created a concept for home food delivery, focusing on the comfort dining at home that replicates the experience of dining out. LOGIC associated the brand with home entertainment, whether the consumer was watching a movie or having dinner with friends or family in their own environment. The concept filled both a gap in the market and a consumer need and was the first product in its category.

Who needs this book?

This book is written for all business owners in our region and to every business owner who has decided to be the CEO of his own firm. My first premise is that a CEO has a job description and certain set of responsibilities and must act as an employee more than the owner of the company. Not all, but most business owners in our region disregard the structures required for successful business practices and instead go forward as he pleases. The end result—the amount of investment wasted—is always shocking. Further, marketing is completely misunderstood by many of the business owners who equate marketing with sales. Without planning or strategy how far can your company grow? Not far in my opinion. This book, therefore, emphasizes the importance of marketing, all its applications and how the CEO or business owners in our region must recognize the importance of marketing and implement its principles.

This book is organized around three main themes: 1) the current market reality for both small- and mid-size companies of the Middle East; 2) the common mistakes and solutions to the Middle Eastern model of marketing, 3) and my model of eccentric marketing, showing how it has worked in Saudi Arabia.

As you continue reading this book, you may experience moments of anger precipitated by my writing. Please bear with my approach and tell me if you think I am justified or not. Many CEOs who read this book will disagree with me on various issues. It is my utmost opinion that the discussion is for their own good, for the sake of their firms and for the sake of the Middle East.

Chapter 1

OUR MARKET REALITY

For purposes of this book, the Middle East includes some parts of northern Africa, and as Arabs, I mean both East and North Africa. This defines our current operating region and our short-term target region. The growing concern is that most firms in our region are small-scale firms, and even under proper development, their growth has been stagnant for a number of years. Much of this stagnation can be attributed to the owner/CEO who will not change his management style or adapt to global trends of business practice, particularly allowing the marketing and finance departments to play a key role of the organization. Further, these companies need an overall structure with a stated mission and vision for both short- and long-term growth.

Let's look at our history for a moment to understand where we are today. In the next chapter, we'll thoroughly explore the role that the CEO/owner plays in the Middle East's business market along with some common marketing mistakes and their solutions.

Commerce and Trade

As Arabs, we were the first people to trade between countries for commodities. Out of the Arab world came the Hadramis from Hadramouth. They traveled to trade with the Far East, as far as Indonesia, and as far west as east Africa. That method of transaction still exists per se; in fact, it forms the majority of business operations in the Arab world. The generic business of trading allows business owners to buy products or services and sell them to the local market or within the market as product exchange. This method of business transaction is as important now as it was in the past in our region.

While *trading and selling* became ingrained behaviors, *producing* was never part of the Arab cultural heritage. Today, we have minimal industries and manufacturing, and produce a minimal number of our own brands. We do, however, form major mergers with foreign firms. This is a bilateral trade exchange, however and I believe the foreign partner is the financially beneficiary of this arrangement. I say this because merger partners tend to have management strategies that include globalization, with the goal of establishing a presence in almost every country with economic purchasing power. It accomplishes globalization via mergers with local operating firms. The local firm benefits by learning the trade, but not by gaining potential penetration outside its area. Trade marketing to me, therefore, is just product dumping, even though the local firm is a licensed representative of the brand within the country. This is not a bad thing if the local firm's basic interest is in gaining financial benefit from their brand within its country. But, at the end of the day, that local firm is just a contracted representative of the brand.

How important is marketing?

How many of our brands are represented in other countries? We can name a few. But having just "a few" doesn't help our future maturity growth. To have a Middle Eastern brands represented in other countries is part of trade, just as being prominent in our regional markets. Countries like the United Arab Emirates and Egypt have seen tremendous recent growth with properly structured business organizations, both in the region and in the international arena.

Here is where the confusion over how businesses view what marketing is. Some think it is sales, while others just consider it purely advertising. Marketing, however, is a very critical set of processes; ones that you will learn by reading this book.

Let's take, for example Orascom Telecom. Headquartered in Egypt, Orascom Telecom is a reputable mobile telecommunication operating company, both in the region and beyond. This firm's initial contact with mobile operating experience was when the Egyptian government decided to privatize its mobile-based company. Mr. Naguib Sawrise, CEO of Orascom, won the bid and thankfully, had a stated vision to operate in numerous countries in the region. Today, Orascom operates in many regional countries as far as Pakistan and its future looks bright. Another example, Vodafone, is based in the United Kingdom and is the largest mobile network company in the world. The brand exists in most Middle Eastern countries, Europe and the Far East. The company's CEO and management have a global strategy: what they sell is the brand name and the expertise. In fact, Vodafone recently merged with a local operating mobile company in Turkey and insisted that the brand name in this region be changed to Vodofone.

These examples show that our potential is enormous, but without the proper structure and operating principles, your company is doomed to fail. Subsequent chapters of this book will explain how business owners must recognize the potential of the region; hire the right employees for the organization; and build and structure their firm to flourish in the local market, regionally and then globally. Your firm must have an adequate plan to deploy all strategies whether it is marketing or financing.

These steps will change our nature of doing business in our region and are models that have worked for other companies. These changes must be made from the roots of how we conduct business today. For example, many grocery and clothing stores are individually owned, with some having chains that represent imported fashion brands. If we rate the growth of each from a future prospective, however, we will find their growth has been a stagnant. This puts our region way behind the rest of the world. If adaptability is accepted and deployed, however, and if professional consultants with proven records begin to assist these owners, they will see their companies flourish. This is a vitally important step in building a company—there must be strong insight to all needs in order to ensure proper growth.

Now that we've identified the overall reality and drawbacks of our market, let's look at some of the common mistakes we make in our region. These mistakes will be accompanied by general corrections that need to be made in order for eccentric marketing to be applied effectively.

Chapter 2

WHAT ARE OUR MISTAKES?
WHAT ARE THE SOLUTIONS?

Marketing is a process in which the product or service is designed, created and continually refined to fulfill the target audience's needs. In today's market, creativity and innovation regarding a concept allows marketing to be completely successful. Business owners must realize that in the Middle East and globally, there are many redundant and competing product brands. The question, therefore, becomes: which of them will survive and thrive?

The answer is simple. The first brand that dominates the consciousness of the consumer will be the survivor. Dominating a consumer category (i.e., a specific age group or perceived life-style) occurs because of marketing and branding. Thus, the importance of marketing in any given organization cannot be taken lightly. Marketing is the heart, the engine, the essential essence if you will that promotes the organization and its products and services.

In our region, however, there are many obstacles that marketing faces, and therefore our brands are not achieving their potential. This section describes the five most common operating procedures, beliefs and practices (or lack of these things) from which our region suffers. After each section, a solution that includes various marketing principles is described.

Mistake #1: Our CEOs Operate "My Way or No Way"

"My Way or No Way" is the basic attitude CEOs in our region hold toward the role of marketing. Owning and running the business and making sales are all about satisfying the owner's ego. If there is to be ego in marketing, it's preferably that the ego is infused with knowledge, rather than just an ego named "My Way." "My Way" is a killer for the potential success of any brand.

It's true that as CEO you must oversee the total business process. But the hard-headed CEO may decide within a second to change the course of the company for personal reasons, rather than for the sake of the business. As the owner and the person responsible for the brand's life cycle, the hard-headed CEO will face decline much sooner because of decisions based on impulsive behavior. The sad fact is that many of our region's CEOs decide the fate of their brands based on personal preferences. The owner's ego and impulsive behavior makes it more important to him to appear high on the totem pole than to nurture the total life of the organization and its objectives. This sad reality is what we face daily.

Another fact of most Arab companies in the region is that they are solely owned by a family. You find that the upper management consists of the family whether they have the experience or not. The decisions made will reflect what the family says rather than actual facts of the market.

There are, indeed, some privately-owned companies today that have hired qualified CEOs to do the job and achieve maximum results. But these companies are scarce. Other owners of privately-held firms with enormous growth potential have decided that since they are the owner, they should be the CEO as well. Apparently a job description and proper qualifications don't apply in this case. Sadly, the risk level can be predicted easily—that business will be gone in no time without a qualified CEO managing the company.

CEO, Don't Cry for Me

Once the business is in trouble, the CEO sits in his office realizing that he cannot be the jack of all trades. He regrets every action he has taken. His actions only took his product or service two blocks away. Unfortunately, he looks back and blames his marketing department for the failure, ultimately firing each and every one of them—only admitting to himself that he is fully responsible for the outcome of his actions. His ego took him so far that he didn't realize he was only listening to his own inner voice. He denied the validity of the professional marketing department that he hired.

So, the brand or company has died and the loss must be absorbed. Brands are like human nature: they go through a life cycle. What's dead can never be brought back to life; that's nature's course. At this stage, all the brand can do is lament: "Dear Mr. CEO: Don't cry for me—you're the reason for my death and failure."

I am speaking from deep within in my heart with the agony of experience. I have seen how some brands completely vanish from the market, due to the hard-headed, egotistical CEO who decides that he is right and that the true process of marketing is wrong. Our regional CEOs often sadly only assume and carry the title, rather than earning it. They never try to understand their responsibility to the brand until reality strikes. Let's look at how we can change this.

Solution #1: Clearly Define Responsibilities

No matter how qualified or unqualified, it's the business owner who decides the fate of his firm. The egotistical owner who decides to be CEO must realize what it really takes to be a CEO, for the sake of his company and for the Arab region—for all who want to go global market with their brands. When the owner of a business also acts as its CEO, all too often he assigns himself the title without understating the explicit details of his job description.

If a CEO can't read between the lines regarding the opportunities that brands present, he should clearly define the responsibilities in the firm and hire experts to fulfill these roles. The owner must be willing to hire and listen to professionals.

The two titles—owner and CEO—have distinguishably different goals. The owner's goal is to set up the company and state the goals for his organization. If the owner is financially capable, but not well-equipped with managerial skills to efficiently run the organization, he should hire a properly qualified, credentialed proxy to operate his organization—a CEO. Doing so will ensure the long-term survival of the company, the owner himself and ultimately our nation.

A CEO has the full-time job of overseeing the overall operation of the organization. He has the commitment and the responsibility to provide success on behalf of the shareholders, and reports directly to the Board. The CEO's job from the start-up of the company is to see the overall company planning and strategy, to delegate, to oversee the company's operations and to ensure efficiency. He is also responsible for approving the company's operational procedures, policies and standards and direct company planning and policy making committee and much more.

In this case, the owner must be modest and manage by overarching objectives in order for our brands to reach the global marketplace. Hard-headed CEOs don't realize the risk to the brand's value until trouble hits. To fix problems at this point is not an easy process, and it's expensive. Instead, the decision on a brand's life should be carefully analyzed, planned and organized in a deliberate way. This process should not be based on assumptions and personal preference, but on facts and market reality in order for the brand to achieve its objectives. The owner must put his ego aside for the benefit of his products and his company.

A few business owners have taken this major step and the move has paid them back properly. Their organizations are able and willing to move forward with their strategy to serve more countries within and outside the region. An example would be Bison, the locally-produced energy drink here in Saudi Arabia. This brand serves the entire region while working its way to serve other regions such as Africa according to a representative from the company.

So what, exactly, is a qualified CEO?

The qualified CEO will ensure that the company is achieving its goals and receiving appropriate rewards. He can establish a proper management strategy to penetrate more assets and raise the total equity of the firm. He will properly hire upper-level managers to assist him in implementing the organizations goals. He will delegate accordingly and see that the total tasks are achieved.

There are many qualified CEOs in our region that can assist in setting up the proper structure for the organization. There are many qualified businesspeople that can ensure that the organization stays intact and self-sufficient. In summary and in my opinion, it's all about levels of self-esteem. If at one point in time the firm is doing quite well and expanding its efforts into new geographical areas, the owner might decide to fire the CEO to save money paying his high salary. In the worst-case scenario, the owner will decide to install himself or his son as the CEO, believing that this will push things forward. The question of this dubious decision is: What will the end result be?

Who will be responsible?

Owners are never responsible in our region; they are intent on believing that they are always right and the rest of the world is wrong. But their responsibility should not just be to their family—it should be to our nation as a whole. Our nation expects business owners to flourish, to support the total mechanism of the local economy, including exports and national branding. The risks involved between being an owner and being a CEO are tremendous. A qualified CEO has the experience to run the organization and reduce its risks. A qualified CEO reduces the chance of shutting down or going out of business. If things are not established clearly, then the company's maturity will never progress, and probably decline. I'm afraid to say that it will operate either only as a small business or it will finally fade from existence.

For a business owner to hire a competent CEO to run the business is a simple idea, but it should be a well-reasoned decision. The question is: are we working for own personal satisfaction or do we have a responsibility to the Middle East region? Do we understand that we must help our nation compete properly in this era of globalization? Are we thinking globally, or just flexing our muscles to satisfy our self-esteem? If the owners of the businesses in our region understand the role of a CEO, then we can expect our businesses to flourish strategically around the globe.

Mistake #2: Operating by Assumption

Many of our brands are built on personal assumptions by those who possess only the lowest degree of basic marketing knowledge. Marketing, however, cannot rest on assumptions, only on facts and innovative ideas. So what, exactly, is "assumption marketing?" Assumption marketing is when the business owner sits with his relatives and friends and decides to buy, import or even produce products *assuming* they will sell in the market based on personal feelings. The owner then decides to produce the product or even import it without understanding his target audience or what segment of the market to which he will address his product. The initial business decision—to decide to produce the product—was based on assumptions, not on market need. His total marketing plan is one big assumption as to who is his direct target audience actually is.

Many small-scale and larger-scale operations have been guilty of using this approach. Assumption has become a process of marketing in our region. This is a very negative trend that has caused us to fall behind the rest of the world. For example, a larger-scale operation that launched its brand thirty years ago may have seen its market share dwindle to a few percentage points simply because its leaders have disregarded the importance of marketing. Despite the small losses over time, these leaders figured that they were doing "well enough" that they should just let things continue "as is." What the CEO typically does, however, is blame the marketing department, even though he hasn't relied on them for guidance. What others do is hire unqualified employees to manage sensitive departments such as marketing. These two problems—blaming a marketing department that has no power and hiring unqualified employees—becomes a vicious cycle. The real question is this, however: Is following an assumption risky to any new or existing brand or idea? The resounding answer is "Yes!" Ask any reputable financial consultant and see what he has to say.

I also have known some big operating plants that were doing a remarkable job regarding production, salaries and benefits. The owner of the operation, however, decided to fire the CEO and have his own son operate it. After taking this ill-advised action, the declining margins of the plants became clearly evident. As more firms operate under this philosophy, sooner or later the existing owner will have to find a new geographical location and find a new target audience.

Solution #2: Operate with Intent, Hire the Right People

Operating with intent and hiring the right people returns us to our discussion of the CEO. First, the qualified CEO will hire those who best fit the firm and its objectives. Establishing the proper qualifications for each position is the most important responsibility in the overall process of his Human Resources department. The qualified CEO will hire be best people who have the qualifications to fulfill the job responsibilities required. For example, like the unqualified owner, the unqualified CEO will hire based on favoritism and assumptions. Often, owners who also act as the CEO hire their own children to such posts as vice president or even as sensitive a position as vice president of marketing. These children may not have the qualifications to help the company thrive and survive.

Operating with intent means to plan and implement marketing strategies. Many of us in this part of the world pay far less attention to marketing than we should. We'd rather focus on the tangible aspects of selling products and services, such as estimating that the total equity of the product lies in its taste or its function. We also wrongly assume that all it takes to beat our competition is to make sure our product is much better. Really, in all decisions related to our brands, we should operate with *intent*—using the principles described later in this book—not on assumptions.

It is my contention that brand marketing should be left to marketers and not to the CEO of the organization. The marketer, to be successful, will be well-equipped with appropriate knowledge and experience. If the business owners do not understand what marketing is, he should hire a firm that will structure the organization properly and deploy the most qualified employees for each job in the structure, especially if the position to be filled is that of CEO.

To avoid assumption marketing at the inception of the company, hire the right players and clearly define long- and short-term objectives. These objectives must be well aligned with the overall company brand objective. We need not look to far see some of companies that operate in the fashion. For example, many local Dubai brands in the United Emirates have broken into the global market. Think of Emirates Air Lines for example. They were a small market player a decade ago, and today they are one of the fastest growing brands in the industry. Why? Ask the CEO. He had a vision and made sure that the brand he created would fulfill its promise. Further, the city of Dubai is a world-wide brand destination for real estate, shopping and life-style. On the business-to-business side, the strongest brands are SABIC and the Port of Dubai.

Are these brands built on assumptions? Not at all! The CEOs of these brands know exactly what their short-term and long-term plans are for their brands. We must avoid the dangerous risks of operating our businesses based on assumptions. Those responsible for ensuring this happens are the business owners or the brand owners, more so than the members of the organization. Still, both groups—top management and employees—need to work together toward common, well-established goals.

SIDEBAR 1: In our own hands

Most CEOs in our region don't listen to marketing experts; rather, they emphasize that they have market knowledge and know how to drive their brands to market to achieve great success.

This is without even a general understanding as to what marketing and its related applications are. Their assumptions lead to a poor effort for the consumer that simply aims to please CEOs' egos with an enormous waste of brand resources.

The basic role of the CEO is to delegate, allowing the marketing department to function according to the markets' needs. Without interference. If an organization is led by one decision-maker who does not assess proper market analyses and who bases policy on conversations while sipping tea with friends, who think that the product will sell, then there are problems. Many carry the title of CEO for prestige without understanding the actual role or exploring what it means.

Some CEOs try to build the identity of a brand without having basic knowledge of what brand identity is and how to use it. This has caused many to decline just as they are launched. Insisting is one thing, but knowing is another. Most think that branding is an external issue directed to the target audience, but the most important aspect of branding is internal, from bottom to top, where each department is presented with the corporate ID and its mission as well as the brands it promotes. This includes the finance department. We all know that successful brands equal cash flow.

The adaptation is simple if the CEO agrees to change, but most inherited their knowledge of business from their forefathers, and they follow in those footsteps while the whole world changes and adopts current trends.

So, if a CEO does not agree to make internal changes, there is no way in the world that our brands would pass the port of Sudan.

There are professional companies that specialize in business-building. These organizations are able to restore a company and show it how to build essential business processes to achieve its objectives. Most CEOs who have met these companies always consider the price rather than looking at the overall opportunities to reshape their companies. If this form of thinking does not change, then we are basically inviting all brands to come and market to our consumers while we sit in our offices and discuss the word of 'globalization,' or whatever.

Help is needed; away from the ego of any CEO who wants to act as a jack-of-all—trades. We must admit our shortcomings and solve them, not modify them because it would hurt egos. We must admit our ability to execute and delegate certain tasks to the professionals we have hired in order to achieve our objectives. Our egos will take us only so far, until the day when we realize that it is too late to correct our mistakes.

I strongly suggest setting up a regional marketing association that will assist all of the organizations that need to market their brands outside our own region. It is vitally important that we take this action as soon as possible in order to build infrastructures properly.

We can't afford to wait; we are already witnessing the influx of foreign brands to our region from different industrial sectors, even if they are created by a merger with a local partnership, they are still considered a foreign brand.

Those foreign brands that are locally produced out-sell any of our local brands by a substantial margin, and this will slow down our efforts to move our companies to new geographical regions and lose the essence of one day being leaders in the global market.

Gulf Marketing Review, June 2007

Mistake #3: We Don't Listen and Adapt

My argument is not completely about the actions of the business owner, as has been discussed to this point. Rather, it is about long-term strategies for our brands to flourish globally. The core of the problem, however, is that the owner of the private business decides to do his own thing, no matter what the risk level is—*he doesn't listen*.

I often sit and wonder why we aren't we listening to those who know a lot more than we do in one way or the other? I consider the biggest risk for the Arab world to be that we will never, ever enjoy a global competitive edge if we don't improve how we think about our business operations. There are times when running a privately-owned, conglomerated organization that we must consider asking those who are *business builders* to assist us. Otherwise, it will be too late for us and we will end up consumers forever.

Some take marketing from a theoretical perspective, in which just opinions are put forth and millions of dollars are invested in the product or service based on that opinion—without clearly identifying who the real audience for their product actually is. Money does not grow on trees, and products will never move off the supermarket shelves unless they are clearly understood by the target audience and suit its needs and behaviors. Be aware of the risk that is involved in disregarding marketing! Take notice of the examples of those who built up proper marketing foundations. The end result is that their brand maintains a healthy cash flow.

Solution #3: Listen to those who know and begin to change

It is imperative that we change our thinking in order to flourish and become producers of mass brands. We must break from tradition and adopt proper organizational structures adaptable to a global economy. We must employ those who know how to assist us in making this shift. This is the only way we will flourish as firms and brands.

We must recognize that the region's trading methodology has changed from the way our forefathers operated; therefore, we must adapt to changes. This willingness to adapt must start with the owner of the operation. This very simple paradigm shift can transport us to higher levels and entrench us in the global market, not just with a few brands, but with more and more. One day we as a region we will be efficiently branded and a recognized global player.

To become a global player, we must listen to our higher leaders. Leaders set examples, and we must follow those examples in order to proceed toward a brighter tomorrow. For example, the Commerce Ministries should provide models for business owners to obtain the required licenses. Most businesses are applying for a general trade license, which is basically about 85 percent of our market today. Retail owners gear themselves to import foreign goods, because local consumers trust the quality of imported goods. If we produce and enforce proper strategies and plans, however, we will also gain consumers' confidence in our products. This applies to many elements of a business. If you have a general trading company, the most important factor is proper marketing plans. Business owners must educate themselves on all aspects of marketing, such as creating their own brands and setting up a proper marketing department in order to achieve overall goals.

This begs the question: why should we stick merely to trade? Things are changing; for the future to be bright, we must do things right today. For example, every decade we face new generations of potential buyers of our consumer brands. If we don't address these new generations and their preferences, we will likely experience a generational decline in business. Future consumers will not act or behave like our forefathers did. They will have their own needs as consumers and old ways of trading will not be forced upon them. The alternative is they move on to well-represented, imported brands because these cater to their needs and behaviors, rather than buying goods produced within the Arab world.

This is the sad reality of how we conduct marketing. We don't accept changes easily; we plod along with habits that we have used for generations. The key, therefore, is adaptability. The new generation is adapting the ways in which their fathers conducted the trade business and it has become a continuous cycle through the generations. This continuity is actually frightening; one day we will be cornered and find that our resources have not been used properly to reach our product's consumers.

Mistake #4: We use the muscle of money the wrong way

Does money wield muscle? Yes, when it's used well for the sake of the company. We can name many brands along these lines—Emirates Airlines, Mercedes, Microsoft and Starbucks are good examples of brands that are well-recognized worldwide and create major cash flow. In our own market reality, however, we consider it a waste of money to create a brand using the proper tools. We concentrate 100% on production and quality of taste for example. But the fact is our consumers don't think the same way as the owner of the company. The owner invests millions of dollars on production and manpower, yet the marketing department consists of salespeople who join the force of *distribution* as described above—push and shove is what I call it.

According to the owner, the plant should perform miracles in term of sales. When asked, "Why you don't consider a proper marketing plan or set up a proper marketing department, fully equipped with manpower and a proper budget?" Their answer is inevitably: "Why spend when I can save?" I don't see how the owner is saving money while his market share is declining. Instead he is losing money, and in the near future he will be faced with selling the company as depreciated equipment.

The other dilemma is the misconception that business owners expect simply advertising to bring about the end result without proper marketing logistics and a clear marketing plan established—or even without a proper brand-building strategy, including positioning and personification. Advertising spending can be enormous, but it does not translate into actual sales. Advertising has become a mindless trend. How can you recover those losses? Sometimes you can't. Once a brand is registered in the consumer's mind as a poorly experienced brand, it's hard to change that perception. And, to rebuild the brand image would also be overly expensive.

Other companies spend millions on brand communication without a proper marketing platform. Whenever you launch a mass consumer product, the plan given to the marketing department is to reach everyone through communication and make sure the product is well-distributed. What happens if these relatively new brands are competing against strong brands that are already dominant in the market? These generic marketers still rely solely on the generic marketing mix and use communication to try to reach ultimate brand results. This approach is completely wrong. If positioning, market segmentation and strategy are not deployed along with a well-planned marketing mix, then you will have problems seeing the brand become a recognizable part of people's lives.

I have seen case after case of this. I have seen many television advertisements for a new brand in the market. Often, there would be nothing different about the "new" brand, except a different name, different color logo and a lame slogan with no clear-cut positioning. What happens next is that the brand will decline gradually until it dies a natural death. The waste generated is not associated with the product alone; it's everything else that was built along with the product.

Solution #4: Use Your Money Wisely

The solution to the mistake of using money in the wrong ways is simple: exert your money muscle during the informative months of a brand's introduction. This is one of the primary reasons why we are still in the early stages of understanding what marketing truly is. We have professional marketers in the region who are ready to assist any owner with their marketing and to help establish their marketing department. It's a crucial process if the owner wishes to attain positive results for his firm. There is a few who follow the proper method of marketing and use their money muscle to capitalize on the brand For example, the real estate giant Emaar, Emirates Airlines and DP World are all brands based in Dubai. I give them credit for how far they have come in their market maturity, and their market penetration has grown geographically. These brands have great potential for widening their scope to new regions outside our own. Already, Emmar operates outside of the region and Emirates Airlines has grown rapidly as well.

There are several ways to use the power of your money including outsourcing and valuing our brands wisely.

Outsourcing

Outsourcing is an excellent way to use your money wisely. China has become a major production hub for both Middle East-branded products and non-branded daily use items. Many of the firms that plan to brand their products for a middle-class audience use China as a production hub. Usually these firms work in the apparel, household items and furniture industries, and outsourcing is beneficial for cost efficiency.

I support outsourcing in cases where a firm plans to invest and capitalize on brands that can penetrate both within the region and outside the region. Efficiency is the key here. There are many advantages to looking elsewhere for cheaper labor that will produce products according to the firm's standards. The United States, for example, has been a key player in the past and present on outsourcing; many major American brands are produced in the Asia-Pacific region. Now, China has become a hub for the Middle East even more so than for the United States. This is due to import restrictions and quotas applied by the U.S. on Chinese textiles and apparel.

Because theses firms have cut costs by outsourcing, they have the money to focus on building their brands. Perhaps the critical question is whether they know how to accomplish this. I believe that there are many brand-building specialists that can help these firms capitalize on their brands. But that's only if the owner of the brand totally understands the brand value.

At times you have seen a foreign retail brand operating in your city and generating enormous traffic. At the same time, the firm's merchandise is made in China. The owner of the competing local brand asks himself "Why is this happening?" The difference is that the foreign retailer invested more in positioning its brands so that it could properly communicate with the target audience, even while outsourcing its merchandize from china or Taiwan. It's quite a simple concept—outsourcing for production is a great way to go, if it can save you money. Money saved on production, then, can be redirected to capitalize on marketing and branding in order to attain and maintain a strong consumer base.

Valuing our brands

U.S. firms' goal in outsourcing is to capitalize their brand assets, while overseeing cost and quality assurance. This allows many of their brands to serve a global market. Most of these firms have marketing strategies for their brands to attract certain demographics of target audiences around the world. Are we in the Middle East heading in that direction? I believe not. Few Arab firms are thinking about, trying to understand and applying models that have worked elsewhere. Some, however, have been successful in adopting new ways of thinking that are resulting from global competition. The major question for these firms in our region related to outsourcing is: Are they capitalizing on their brands? Or are they still confused about the brand's value?

Many tend to believe that simply a logo will do the job, rather than aligning the total brand with consumer needs, building its personality, and differentiating their brands from their competitors.

Mistake #5: We lack innovation.

Do we really lack innovation? The sad answer is yes. We have a well-equipped society, but many of our innovators travel abroad to fully realize their dreams. Marketers in our region are fully equipped to implement the total marketing process and create successful brands. The problem is not with the marketers—it's with the owners of the firms. A publicly-shared company does not have this problem in our region, but how many of those exist? Not many—the majority of firms are privately owned and most of those are small-scale firms. Growth comes when the brand is adequately competitive and well-built. Unfortunately, we lack the tendency to regard the brand as a source of income. And, without the proper awareness of the brand, it's hard for the product to reach distributors.

Further, our pattern has been to move quickly to copy a success story; in a few months to a year following a successful brand, you will find six to seven other brands trying to copy the success story of the first. The funny thing is that most of the newcomers' board members will sit and discuss market share—is their market share growing, or are they spending enough on advertising to increase market share by 5%? How much money will you need to dump on advertising to gain market share? If you spend millions, how will you earn a return?

These are not necessarily the right questions to ask. As I've already established, the marketing department in some of these companies is good for nothing. That's because their understanding of marketing is basically limited to appearing in every medium possible, whether or not that medium truly targets their core audience. They go simply for what they call "presence." Think of a brand like Starbucks. It's a mega-brand known worldwide. Do you see advertisements for it everywhere? Hardly! Yet you see Starbucks stores everywhere; in major cities, you can probably see the stores on every other block.

Unfortunately, we take the world of marketing, creativity and innovation very lightly. We often consider a brand just a logo printed on a printing press. A brand is much, much more than that. And, gentlemen, if you are reading this book, you must admit you have realized that the overall marketing process in today's world is a lot different than during the days your forefathers were trading. Copying other models does not assist us in breaking into the global market. It demonstrates a complete lack of innovation and failure to build an idea with proper marketing models.

On one occasion—I have witnesses—an investor asked me to replicate something he saw working in the local market. It was the dominant brand in the market and I decided there was no way I would put my neck on the line. The brand was the first in the category and was known for its strong selling propositions. It was well-registered with its target audience—enough so that when you mentioned the brand name, the average consumer could tell you what the product line entailed. I sat in my house and thought about my conversation with this investor. What was he thinking? Why didn't he want to become a dominant brand leader in another area, rather than trying to break into a market where he knew that he didn't have a chance?

Solution #5: Keep our innovators home!

Innovation is what will help us advance our brands. When we think of building brands, we invite people from overseas firms to assist us. They bring with them their own innovations. The question is: When will we be innovators ourselves? When will an innovation be 100% our own? When will we differentiate and succeed in creating something that the whole world needs?

I ask myself these questions almost every day. What we have to do is to create what is needed. We have an opportunity—a huge opportunity—to become a global player. Keep our innovators at home! Give them the chance to excel, and our region will begin to see the difference. One day we will have locally-created brands that will serve the global market. Think about this concept carefully and we can create brands that will bowl the world over in a wide variety of industries. What we need to do is attain results.

So what strategies should you implement to address your target audience and fulfill their needs?

It's all about market planning and the level of risk business people are willing to take. Most investors are risk-takers, but they have to have proper insight into the market to take even a minimal risk. As mentioned, a "good" risk is calculated as one that copies something else that has been successful. That is the most risk many are willing to take and, really, it's not even minimal. Our region is not risk-oriented to new ideas. Many won't even try to create a new category; they'd rather work with what exists. This is why we are so limited to a just a few industries. For example, if you sell a car, then that's a great business. But a few years later you may see a million other car dealers and agents popping up around the region. The same applies for other products.

And, it's only when things go wrong that experts are called in to clean up the mess. As a marketer, however, it is very hard to resurrect a dead brand. The better approach would be let it die and start anew, primarily because a dead brand means that the consumer has already had a bad experience and is not likely to give it another try. Ultimately, however, the next steps have always been the owner's call. He is the one, and the only one, who decides the fate of the brand. With this being the case, many owners are asking: "Why are we not penetrating the global market? Why are we not competitive with our foreign counterparts?" These questions can only be answered by the owner of the brand, who is, at the same time. the CEO—whether you like it or not. Things are very forceful in the market; once it's decided, things move until brands are dead. It will keep happening until you ask the owner to step aside, earn the money and let those who are professionals do their job. If these changes are not made today, while we are ready for it, then forget our future and the future of our generations to come.

Start being innovative by realizing that things change everyday; consumers change and new generations are born after other generations. How do we carry on? I would plainly say focus, innovate and be trendsetters. Today's brand mechanisms involve a vigorous psychoanalysis on consumer behavior and changes, but it all revolves around two main fundamentals: consumers' visual perception and their emotional bond to the brand. Innovation and creativity are the cornerstones of eccentric marketing, so keep reading!

Chapter 3

MARKETING 101:
THE GENERIC FOUR PS AND MARKETING MIX

I start this section with a bold statement: ***the importance of marketing in 100% locally-owned firms in our region of the Arab world is still disregarded.*** I have demonstrated this in the preceding chapter discussing the mistakes we make and how these mistakes can be resolved. Now that we know what mistakes we make and the general solutions to those issues, this chapter will establish the foundation for eccentric marketing.

What we know as Marketing 101, or the basic principle of marketing, are the famous Four Ps—Product, Place, Price and Promotion—which Neil Borden introduced as "the marketing mix" during his presidential address to the American Marketing Association. The four P's or marketing mix are the basic ingredients of marketing. Combined, these elements work together to implement marketing strategies. The four Ps are:

- **Product** is the object or service you would like to introduce to your target audience.
- **Place** is the location of your business or the location where you want your product or service to be distributed or placed.

- **Price** is what you wish your customer to pay for your product, which depends on competition, brand value and you target customer's income.
- **Promotion** is the communication tools you use between the product and consumer, which includes advertising, word of mouth and point of sale.

I know many may disagree with me calling these principles the *generic* four Ps, or more commonly, marketing mix. These are the basic principles of marketing, however, and many of us have encountered these principles in our university years. Are they important today? The resounding answer is "Yes!" The more important question, however, is *how* important are they? It is my contention that if we base everything on the market mix as an operating factor of marketing within our organization, we have a problem—a major problem. Therefore, for our region, I suggest some adjustments to the Four Ps as they are normally taught in school.

The marketing mix is only the basic foundation for applying marketing applications. Creativity and innovation must be added to this basic foundation in order to implement eccentric marketing. It's sad that many regional firms stop at the basic marketing mix and do not infuse their marketing with creativity and innovation. For example, calculate the monetary value of sixty salesmen fighting their way through a tight market or category. Things become so cluttered that the cost of the marketing department outweighs the total income generated In this case, the lack of innovation and creativity holds the brand back.

Instead, realize that consumers expect changes and trends, especially the younger audience. Marketing applications are continuously growing as more marketers act innovatively to attain end results for their brands. New strategies—those that include innovation and creativity—are ways in which you can break loose from your competition. These include your total communication strategy to introduce your brand to the market.

Marketing mix plus innovation equals brand success. Imagine the market as a platform where brands are like livestock running around trying to gain confidence and growth. The brands that are not well-raised and fed by their guardians are likely to die during their formative years.

Now that we have established that the marketing mix is the basic platform for your overall marketing planning, what's the next step? When will we realize the importance of total marketing as the engine of the business? When will we be able to realize that our shortcomings are purely marketing issues?

Let's look in general at the four P's and how the Middle East can add creativity and innovation to each piece of their marketing mix.

Let me start by giving you some specific examples of **product categories**. The dairy product milk is a category, carbonated drinks are a category and local and imported produce is also a category. Once you have identified your category, ask yourself some questions:

- How cluttered is your consumer product category?
- Are consumers given many choices with your category?
- What is the market share of the companies who are massively penetrating this category?
- What is the total target population within each category? Can you observe the total population?

- What if the category serves only about 8% of the total population? Is that substantial enough to support several brands from different companies?

Each category can include the original concept or the stamp of the brand's creator, but what we witness in our region is a overcrowding of brands within the same category. They are all targeting the same audience with the same key word as a slogan. The prefect example of this in our region is the fresh milk category originated by Al Marai. This company actually "owns" the fresh milk category and identified its product as fresh milk. Others joined the category over time, and today we have five to six brands in the same category—but they do not differentiate themselves. The category has become tight and the consumer will likely set his mind on the first or second brand that was launched.

Once you've answered these questions about your product, it is more important to think about which segment of the consumer market you are targeting. A category can contain many segments of a target audience. For example, some companies may target a demographic of women in their thirties or forties. Others could target the demographic of pregnant women. Each segment is homogeneous in their behavior and needs, so they might respond quickly to a given marketing strategy.

CASE STUDY 1: Milking it for all it's worth

Can long-life milk preserve its shelf-life as fresh products become more popular?

In Saudi Arabia, dairy products have become one of the fastest-moving and most progressive industries in the country. We have witnessed the influx of new players, particularly in the fresh milk and long-life milk (UHTJ) categories.

Saudi Milk by Sadafco was the first to pioneer UHT milk and has been a dominant player for years. Al Marai dominates the fresh-milk sector by far; while fellow brands continue share the gains. Demographically, the majority of fresh-milk consumers are between 25–40 years old, which constitute the majority of the population.

Aided by a strongly endorsed media campaign promoting healthier lifestyles, a changing climate of health awareness and the desire for fewer preservatives, fresh-milk consumption has jumped to the top-selling position, over and above long-life milk products.

The key factor supporting Al Marai's' ever-growing market share in the fresh milk category is because Al Marai is the first to create the fresh milk category, while other brands have lagged behind changes in both trends and environmental needs.

Generally, organisations tend to give marketing less attention in favour of the value of marketing-need studies. Will the long-life milk category eventually fade away? Realistically this is possible due to the enormous worldwide pressure on health awareness and health-education campaigns infiltrating the satellite channels.

Consumer awareness is creating a demand for natural ingredients, fewer additives and fewer preservatives than those being added to extend the shelf life. Ironically, in the daily-use milk category, we have recently witnessed many consumers shifting from long-life milk to fresh milk. Within the next 10 years, the industry will no doubt witness a great change as the present trend of health-conscious consumers develops and grows.

The name Al Marai conjures up the image of fresh milk in consumers' minds. Since other brands have failed to create any individuality, they make the same claims as Al Marai fresh milk, therefore promoting the fresh-milk category which Al Marai created. This has helped Al Marai to increase its sales and widen the category versus long-life milk.

While these brands have become dominant in the market, they concentrated on different categories within the dairy products. The extension has not helped much, but it did leave consumers with choices to identify market share gain for the companies.

Al Marai outsells the category of milk both fresh and UHT, but does it does not sell as much in all other dairy product categories, because the consumers' initial union with Al Marai is fresh milk. The extension from fresh milk to long life milk, juice, cheese and other dairy products has gained Al Marai some market share, but not as the dominant player.

The human mind has a specific space of memory, and not everything seen as products under one brand name will be remembered. The rule of thumb states that a company should concentrate on one product and one brand name, and increase market penetration, instead of having a product line extension under one brand name.

Take, for example, the mind in action; while on a grocery run to buy eggs and milk, your wife calls and asks you to also pick up cheese. As you walk along the supermarket aisles, you have the mindset to buy the brand of milk that you have always seen in your refrigerator, the one that has stared you in the face every morning over coffee.

In the cheese section, you have the brand name for cheese in your mind, and that's what you will buy. Consumer psychology involving brands extension must always be taken into consideration.

Each brand should be known for what it provides and stands rather than for the 20 product extension lines under same umbrella.

I am sitting here in my office faced with a chorus line of 50 varied products, all falling under one brand; however, as I am human, my specific space for memory will only permit me to connect with the original product, that I first experienced and not the 49 that followed.

Bearing this in mind, we should direct our short-term and long-term vision toward a brand life cycle, and focus on creating the ultimate experience and an ongoing emotional union for the consumer. Treat your brand the way you treat yourself—as an individual.

Gulf Marketing Review, March 2007

How far can a category expand to meet the needs of a particular segment? Not very far. A category is like a nation—if the nation cannot meet certain needs of the population, then that nation starts introducing things like home planning awareness according to that country's economical scale. Like nations, everything has a limit and a boundary. You can stretch a brand, but if the category is meant to be stretched then you'll need to explore new geographical markets. To penetrate the same market means to be aware of its limit. We have to accept that our consumers are well aware of their needs and we must consider those needs in order to realize that there are limits. Thus, we must consider segmentation because it gives us a wider scope for differentiation and reaching a wider audience.

Your product category and consumer segment will determine your *place* and *promotion* strategies. It doesn't help to place your product in a discount store if you are creating a luxury brand for high-income consumers. Likewise, it doesn't help to gain endorsements from someone in the juice industry if your product is a chauffer service. These examples may seem overly simplistic, but you'd be amazed at how often business owners ignore these considerations. As I've mentioned, my opinion is that *pricing* should not necessarily be part of your marketing mix. It can become a factor in segmenting products however, as you define your brand profile and the social class for which your brand is intended.

If we have a problem seeing your produce in a particular category, then why not create a category and build on it? The Middle East is very limited in our industrial offerings—most markets are composed of up to 85% consumer-goods retailers. That's why we have more retail banking, and the numbers of those retail banks are growing according to need. It makes a lot of sense. It's a given that we have high spending per capita, but consumers like to explore and experience new trends. The newer generations are different from the older generation. What my dad likes is not the same as what I like, and what my son likes is not the same either.

So how do we go beyond the generic Four Ps and marketing mix to extend the reach of our brands?

Chapter 4

GO BEYOND 101 WITH ECCENTRIC MARKETING

What is Eccentric Marketing?

Eccentric marketing is the value added to what marketing is today, with all of its applications. Eccentric marketing takes your brand a step ahead, treating it like a living entity that seeks out and aspires to join your target audience. Philosophically, eccentric marketing includes:

- The mind, which is the cornerstone of consumers' buying behavior.
- The eye, which is the way your consumers perceive your brand's personality.
- The heart, which is the emotional bond to the brand after the brain makes its decision and registers.

In short, what the *eye sees*, the *mind buys*, and the *heart feels*.

Taken together, these elements create the total outlook of the brand. Succinctly, eccentric marketing is about market innovation, creating a living brand with an emotional relationship to the target audience. By innovation, I mean using creativity to open a new category, or even using strategies directly opposite of what your direct competitors are deploying. The main thought fueling the end result of eccentric marketing, therefore, is that no brand needs to fight for market share. Rather, a brand can dominate a new category as the first brand in that category and set forth a new era.

Once a perception is established, the mind decides whether or not to purchase your product. The heart, or the emotion associated with your brand, the sentiment to be more exact, is the long-lasting union between the brand and the target audience. As long as the brand continues to be innovative and identifies itself with the audience, the union continues to bond.

Eccentric brands fulfill a *need*. Let's consider some existing "needed" brands:

- Atkins is a needed brand for the health conscious consumer. Atkins was the first company to introduce nutritional chocolate bars and shakes that traveled the opposite road of every other product in the category that contained high sugar. Instead, Atkins focused on healthy and nutritional facts to move the brand into the life of a health-conscious target audience. This is a fast-growing audience, one of the fastest actually. Companies that can reach this audience with products containing less sugar, more fiber, but still great taste will flourish. The "need" in this case is to enjoy a great shake or candy bar with nutritional and health power and less the calories.
- Red Bull is another wonderful example. Red Bull is a needed brand for those who seek energy. This was the first beverage in its category to introduce the energy drink, a "need" for the active, alert and adventurous audience.
- Xerox is another example and is a great world brand for those who need copy paper and machinery to make copies. Xerox was the

first to introduce the copy machine concept and it is the dominant brand in the copy category. Xerox fulfills people's needs for copying documents whether in the office, school or home.

- Evian mineral water is a needed brand for product confidence. Evian was the first purified water presented as a world brand, giving people the choice to drink portable, treated water over regular tap water. Many areas of the world need a cleaner and more confidence source of water as opposed to public service water.

Success is the end result for all these brands. Each of these brands was the first in its category and they were built based on the target audiences needs: eat healthy candy bars, photo copy important papers, be alert without drinking coffee, drink cleaner water from a trusted source. These are needed brands that have become essential in the lives of their audience.

Let me bring this philosophy to a level that can be implemented on a practical, day-to-day basis. Eccentric marketing includes two core concepts. The first concept is innovation—breaking through the repetitive brands that are furiously fighting for market share. The second concept is market segmentation—the core skill of identifying a certain demographic (a target market) around which you can build your brand.

In summary, with eccentric marketing a brand becomes lively and fulfills the target audience's needs. It's all about creating products that fill a space or gap in the market. Beginning with that need, all creative processes take place, including creating a business model to mold the idea into a brand. That brand will eventually be able to sustain itself as a living thing. We all know that not every idea is a good idea, but with eccentric marketing you thoroughly examine the idea through a business model using standard marketing applications to see how you will generate revenue.

With this foundation in mind, let's take a closer look at the elements of eccentric marketing.

The Elements of Eccentric Marketing

The tools of eccentric marketing consist of: 1) differentiating your product; 2) building a proper profile of the brand so that it is linked emotionally to the target audience; 3) identifying a certain segment of the market for your brand; and 3) addressing that segment by infusing your product with emotional attributes and deploying proper marketing strategies. Let's look at each element in detail.

1. Differentiate

One of the most important concepts of eccentric marketing is to differentiate your idea, your brand and your total strategy from the other products in your category. Differentiation means communicating with the consumer that your brand exists and that your brand has its own look, feel and personality. Brands that are well differentiated come from business owners who have communicated the intrinsic values, culture and personality of the brand. Therefore, competitors cannot copy them. If you don't differentiate, you will end up at the end of the road.

Imagine you are running to a store to buy milk. You find that every brand looks alike, feels alike, and tastes alike. There is no differentiating factor aside from the names. You will end up buying the one you have always been buying.

If a newcomer brand of milk wishes to enter this tight category, competing for the same demographic and psychographic, what do companies in our region do? They use the ***price factor*** as the differentiating element—always estimating that a lower price is the best buy. In some cases this is true, but is this a sustainable strategy? When you consider offering your product at a lower price, there are other elements you must drop as well: the basic standard of the milk, the look and feel of the packaging and the way you communicate your brand's availability to your audience. Is a lower price therefore a differentiating factor? The answer is "No"—you're basically targeting the lower-income segment of the market and sacrificing your product in the meantime.

When we talk about differentiating, we are talking about the total brand—its life and its positioning with the consumer. Many brands that are still working offer unique selling propositions. Let's take the example of a milk brand again. It may have the same look and feel as all the other brands, but a differentiating point is that the maker has added a certain vitamin ingredient to the milk. That's a good start, but the total brand still has nothing clearly different about it. That's because the company failed to differentiate the packaging— the brand look and the brand personality. The differences must permeate the entire brand—the product, its packaging and its appeal to the audience.

To help me think about differentiation, I imagine myself in the place of the consumer. Consider this scenario:

I am walking down a supermarket aisle, faced with arrays of brands that all look alike. How will I come to experience a particular brand? By name? No. The quality? Well, they all claim to be quality products, so I'll *have to buy almost every brand to experience what each is like. I end up buying the brand that was **first** in its category.*

Because one brand was first in the category, then that brand is the dominant decision factor at this point in the consumer's mind. Returning to our milk example, Al Maari Milk was the first brand in the Saudi fresh milk market. It differentiated itself from long-life UHT milk. In order to be dominating, the second brand must position itself differently than the first product in the category. Differentiating is a must in order to relate the brand to the target audience if all the brands have the same positioning and same claim, such as "quality," which is a dominant propensity in our region.

If the marketing department thinks it can sell a product based only on the concept of "quality," ask them to think again—unless you plan to spend millions of dollars just to prove this claim. Instead, we must think about the product and say what makes it different? What makes it eclectic? What do the competitor's offer and how can we differentiate in the total utility of the brand? These are the questions that are first phase of differentiating your brand from others. Consumers will respond to your efforts and spread the word. Eventually, third parties will endorse the brand.

Not every company has a huge budget for advertising and I address this in the next chapter. Advertising is actually just a claim, often one that consumers do not trust. Instead, they will trust claims from friends, family, co-workers or even a simple newspaper article endorsing the brand. The way to achieve these endorsements is to differentiation your brand, which will grab the consumer's attention and lead many to experience your brand. As I explain later, I believe in the power of public relations over advertising to promote your brand. In less than a year, you will have established your total marketing goal.

2. Create a brand profile.

Think about how good you personally want to look. We all strive to look good in most aspects of life. Many of us work hard to attain recognition, good health and career success. It is the fact of life that we all strive to do well. It's also a fact of life that some succeed and some don't. But overall, how you look, act, speak and behave are all part of your personal "brand profile." A product is no different than a person, and a brand profile should be built according to the needs of the intended target audience. Image matters here. The color scheme matters. Each color has its own meaning for the target audience. The overall outlook of the brand includes direct deliverables that are properly communicated to your audience.

I'm asking you to think about yourself because brands are like humans in that they communicate silently. To attract a large target audience, they can present themselves as a walk of fame. In eccentric marketing, the brand profile is an essential piece of the process. We must study the brand identity properly and position that product to suit its audience. We oversee the processes, contribute the proper colors to the identity and in due order the brand presents itself to the consumer.

It is also important to test every element of the brand profile before presenting your product fully. This will help you gauge the consumer's emotional attributes and the perceptions. It's a bit like marriage—when you meet the person you might want to have as a life partner, there are many elements of the person's profile you consider. When you first see a person, you gain an image of their "packaging."

As you experience that person, however, you gain an "inside" view of the person—her emotional attributes. Many consider the initial profile as the primary element—the rest comes later during the experiences you share before marriage takes place.

Branding is the same way. We get married to brands; we are struck by their profiles and their propositions. Many of us consider those first feelings of attraction to be the core of the profile, even when we get married or involved in a relationship. The essence of the brand profile, however, has multiple meanings to the consumers. It is the first impression, however, that is the most lasting impression. From this first impression grows the connective tissue where the brand starts to become part of the consumer's life. So is brand profile important? Very much so; without it you don't have a place to start.

3. Define and understand your target audience

Although differentiation and a brand profile are critical, they are not a complete solution to branding. We live in a market of multiple social classes. This is where the concept of market segmentation is applied. Considering the nature of the social tiers with which we are presented, it is important to be aware of the social customs and mores of the targeted group. The definition of something in group "A" may be the complete reverse in group "B." Everything from colloquialisms to delivery must be fashioned to appeal to that particular audience in turn giving the brand a sense of familiarity and belonging to the group.

To identify the target audience for eccentric marketing and link the brand to that audience, we must build from an idea. We must determine how this idea is associated with the target audience as a business model. For example, when I first thought of eccentric marketing, I identified the audience that would best benefit from the concepts of the eccentric marketing world. My demographic is between the ages of 16 and 45 and their psychographic is middle-, upper-middle and upper-class. This demographic is both male and female; educated enough to understand the meaning of the brand, and diverse enough to envision how a product can be differentiated. For eccentric marketing, the audience's understanding of branding is the most important element prior to building up the brand and all that goes with it.

To create an eccentric brand, therefore, you must gain a solid sense of your audience. You are about to start a trend and you are expecting a lot of people to follow. You have to read your audience well; discern their preferences both on a social level and an inner level. Usually those who are attracted to eccentric brands are go-getters and trend followers; they can create their own way of life. Even if they are part of a larger society, they are leaders who can transform the whole society to the trend that is being set.

The beauty of understanding the target audience lies not just in facts revealed by research groups. Conducting a focus group, for example, is basically aimed at understanding the behavior and discovering the needs of your target audience. Determining a need is not as simple as conducting a focus group—a need is never just born. A need is never just searched for. Rather, a need is the vital link between the brand and the consumer. Never underestimate the intelligence of your consumers and their ability to understand their needs! Therefore, know your audience and link the brand to their needs. All of this is part of eccentric marketing.

Building the emotional attributes of the brand for your intended audience is like creating a beautiful musical. How eccentric marketing uses all the senses to reach the audience is discussed in the next section. There's nothing magic about it; however, it's just simply understanding and fulfilling the audiences' needs. Some may think that analyzing your audience is unnecessary, but this is not true. With different types of products, we address different segments (i.e., perceptions, preferences, needs, etc.) of the audience and develop the brand according to those perceptions and preferences. Developing a brand is not about what we as sellers like or prefer. Instead, eccentric marketing focuses on what distinct groups within society like and prefer. Each segment has different tastes, different social issues and different interests. These groups exist in massive numbers in our society and around the globe. And, the number of potential customers is growing as the world grows smaller due to the internet, traveling and diverse cultural interactions.

4. Create perceptions that will sell the brand

When something is visually appealing, the mind becomes set and the bond of emotion begins to develop. This is called perception. Brands are about perceptions: if perceptions are missing, you'll have a problem building your brand.

Let's look at an example. You go out for dinner and open the menu. Before you begin to read the details describing each dish, your eyes guide you from item to item, veering toward things that look good to you. Once you spot an image that mesmerizes you, you decide to read the description. If the description is tantalizing, the mind has made its decision. When the time comes to taste your selection, that's where the bond occurs. Based on the actual experience, you begin to create either a sense of union or of dislike with the particular dish you have decided to try.

Eccentric marketing works in this exact way: it focuses on brands the will make a strong impact on perceptions, such as the appearance and taste of a particular menu item. I correlate perceptions to traveling: sound waves travel through air, water travels between nations and wind travels everywhere—basically everything travels. Once your consumer sees an image of something, if that image doesn't travel to his mind then you have a problem. Once a consumer's eye spots the name or the total profile of the brand, the link begins and the whole brand's outlook travels to the consumer's brain to make an impact. Eventually a simple touch of the hand is placed on the brand, and that's where the bonding begins to take place. It is ironic how well it works. This is why perception is one of the five most important elements of eccentric marketing. It's simply a way of life to use your senses to experience the world around you—your eyes, your nose, your tastes, and your touch.

On the contrary, imagine a brand that is not appealing in its overall profile. What are the chances that perceiving it will convince the consumer to initiate an emotional link? Realistically, there's almost no chance for an unappealing brand to create that connection, unless it carries a bargain price. In that case, the decision is not based on perception, but rather how much it costs and how long the product will last. Indeed, low price is considered a perception, especially if the target audience is part of a lower-income group. The cost of building an eccentric brand, however, is more expensive than targeting brands to lower-income citizens. So, for eccentric marketing to be effective, perception must rest on the brand profile. This means that the product must appeal to all the senses—it must look good, taste good, smell good, feel good, all depending on the product. Price may be a secondary consideration if the brand trend is set for that dimension.

Some will argue that price is also a perception. I totally agree that it is. But price will be a secondary consideration for your consumer if your brand fulfills a need and if its total profile is in place. When you go shopping for fast consumer goods, or any commodity, or if you are the right target audience of eccentric marketing, your first experience is the perception of how the brand looks. You will then travel to the brand to experience the perception you have about the brand. Once you have a feel for the brand, the brand has about an 80% chance of actually being purchased.

Another element of perception is the consumer's lifestyle. Does the brand profile fit the lifestyle of the target audience? If it does, you have established an effective perception. If not, it is unlikely that the brand will penetrate the mind of the intended audience; they just won't notice it. That is why it is essential to look at the product and its audience during a total creative process in the initial phase of the building a life for the brand. The total creative process builds the brand so that the impact of perception can be very strong.

5. Infuse total emotional attributes

So, how do we build a brand and how do we build perception of the brand? For a brand to be durable in the market it must now be infused with total emotional attributes. I truly believe in the emotional union between the brand and its user. As we all aspire to have meaningful emotional relations with family and friends; so too does the emotional factor relate to a brand. The total brand individuality can be responsible for creating the emotional link between itself and the consumer. Consumers' emotional bond with the brand can preserve and transform it into a living entity.

Brands must leave an impression of their total outlook and experience. I have mentioned many times that brands are like humans. The consumer can create a love or hate relationship based on the brand's outlook and actual experience with the brand. Eccentric brands, through their fundamental elements, must make sure that the target audience will experience a strong emotional pull and that the total brand outlook will leave a lasting impression. The total emotional contribution from the brand to the consumer can drive the brand to be part of the consumer's lifestyle.

Infusing total emotional attributes means that the brand is consistent in fulfilling the exact emotional needs of the consumer. Once the union is made, the brand has to be consistent in its elements. It has to maintain how the consumer experienced it the first time. The brand must keep focused and consistent; once a drift away from expectations begins, the consumers' dislike may begin to form, and it will be very difficult to bring them back to the brand or fix the mistake. For some, the emotions are gradually grown; however, some consumers have an instant love of the brand. All these situations push the brand further. In sum, emotions are important from the first impression, but the continuity of the relationship between the brand and the audience can involve love or hate. All of these responsibilities are in the hands of the brand owners who are responsible for creating consumer pull through emotional attachment.

Do emotions influence the brand life beyond differentiating it? Definitely yes—invest all your important human senses into the brand and these emotional attributes will act as your agent. The brand will perform according to the target audience's desire and it will be consumed with love and pleasure. Pleasure outsells any category. Whether the pleasure is for need or comfort, it is a pure desire. The consumer will not just purchase your product once, but will be a repeat customer. For a brand owner, this means substantial cash flow and market share gain.

When we look into the deeper side of our consumer base, the most empowering part of our society is emotion. As Arabs we are a strong, emotion-based society. We stick fast to our emotions more so than do those in other parts of the world. Nevertheless, in the overall world population, emotion has a strong impact on a brand and can help a brand outsell its competitors. The more consumers can express their emotions through the brand, the more drastically the total audience will grow. By the same token, one bad experience with the brand can spread hate for that brand everywhere, and the brand's lifecycle will start to decline. It will then begin to age quickly as the firm reduces costs because the sales don't equal the revenue generated.

Brands are truly a created reality. But they are a created reality that all of us enjoy and would love to live with and demand as consumers if we can afford it. Although the mind controls the spending, it's the emotions that make our consumers spend much more on something they love.

6. Mind the consumer's mind and perceptions

The feel of the brand, its total emotional attributes, at times can actually be non-emotional when it comes to a certain need, which creates a demand impact. Emotions can build the strongest path to brand loyalty, but others consider brand loyalty from the perspective of need. Your hope should be that the brand gains consumers' confidence, and yes, confidence is part of brand loyalty.

Loyalty and confidence are more about the mind, however, than raw emotion. Once the mind decides something, it's hard to change it.

The mind is the logical cornerstone of the buying process. At times, however, the emotional attributes of the brand can override the brain's logic. Looking into the deeper side of the consumer audience and analyzing what you find will make it easier to generate success for a brand.

How the brand is positioned in the mind of the consumer is another aspect of eccentric marketing. I highly recommend the book *Positioning: The Battle for Your Mind* by Al Rise and Jack Trout. This is a masterpiece, a breakthrough work on what marketing is today. Am I endorsing them? Absolutely! They are my mentors; I look up to them and their work. In fact, they inspired me to develop the concepts of eccentric marketing.

Your consumers' minds are not something to take lightly, because the mind creates the vital process of marketing that leads to total brand penetration. What the consumer's mind says determines how products will move. The consumer's mind, however, cannot function without perception. Therefore, you must reach consumers' minds through proper brand communication and the total utility of the brand. This communication will transform your product from intangible to tangible—something that the consumer will live with and experience at home, at work and in social outings.

Create a brand, fill the gap, reach the consumer and let it register in the mind and life of the consumer. When you see advertisements or read endorsements, you will remember those related to the brands that are relevant to you. You will ignore those that don't deliver a clear understanding of the brand. The mind, therefore, is accepting what it wants and rejecting things that do not suit it.

Think of individuals. Imagine you see a group of people dressed all the same, as in uniforms, for example, but one person is completely different from all the others. Each person says his name. As an audience member you will likely only remember the name of the person who was dressed differently. This is perception. The mind will only register what was perceived and accepted visually.

This example also applies to brands—those that are differentiated will break through to the consumer's mind. For example, say you are in the supermarket and walking down the beverage aisle. You will have an instant reaction to something your eyes perceive as different. The mind starts the process, aligning it with what you have perceived, and you find yourself walking toward the brand you see as different. The decision to buy this different brand is an important process of the brand, but perception plays the biggest role here. If you are blindfolded, can the mind decide which brand to pick? The clear answer is no!

Chapter 5

ECCENTRIC MARKETING IN ACTION

In this next section, I will answer the most commonly asked questions about eccentric marketing and how they are applied to branding.

Is eccentric marketing really a new dimension?

Eccentric marketing is definitely a new dimension. It offers a new way for brands to come alive and live up to their promises. Everything about eccentric marketing is innovative, and the heart of its creativity lies in its total marketing applications. It is the new dimension that consumers are looking for and what eccentric marketing aims to deliver.

Look around you—how many brands are redundant? Can you see that consumers are fed up with all the advertisements they see on their televisions? Marketing campaigns are boring and advertising agencies are lost in the middle. Same day, same story. Often, no one considers the total needs of the consumer and what will make a difference to them. But this is what brings sales in. If you are not convinced, keep doing what you have been doing. You need to break through the plateau. You need your brand to set a trend—and that trend can never be set without a proper creative process and proper business models to generate revenue.

The target audience of eccentric marketing generally wants to differentiate itself in terms of social class, identity and geographical location. Sad to say, not everything can mix and match. That's a reality that we all face. Creating this new dimension in marketing means you have to set what has not been set, to create what can be easily sold—without the support of 80,000 salesmen. Brands are ready to run, to jump and break through and live—but only if they are properly built according to the emotions, perceptions and decisions of the audience and not according to the assumptions of company CEO.

When we think we know what we like, we make a choice. Some of us follow a personal choice, but the fact is that some just love to follow trends and to fit in with society. There are many segments of consumers, however, and you cannot target all of them because you cannot cater to everyone's likes and tastes. That's why eccentric marketing focuses on certain products for a certain target audience, to ultimately create the new dimension that is needed.

What products respond to eccentric marketing?

The best forum to which eccentric marketing can be applied are consumer goods that target upper-middle and upper-class citizens, including lifestyle and "fast" consumer goods. This industry is broken into segments from food and beverage to all kinds of lifestyle products, such as clothing and leisure products. The basic fundamentals of eccentric marketing require properly investing in the total outlook for the brand. When you think of eccentric marketing, you need to think of the total output the brand will create and the total perception of the target audience.

Eccentric marketing, therefore, is a strong consumer-based marketing model and not a business-to-business model. Eccentric marketing works for the aforementioned industries through *consumer emotions, perceptions and decisions*. Thus, eccentric marketing focuses on which products to promote and how to bring them into the consumer's consciousness. Eccentric marketing products are not generally differentiated by price.

We can alter the eccentric marketing model to fit other products. For example, some industrial brands that lack die-hard creativity such as industrial building products, respond well to eccentric marketing. But it is not business-to-consumer, or as I love to call it, *brand*-to-consumer. I use this phrase because what sells is the brand and not necessarily the business. We all know that brands are business, but what actually sells to the consumer is the product brand.

This is just an overview of industry applications that work with eccentric marketing. It is hard to tamper with or drift from your main focus; once you are focused you will attain the ultimate results for your brands or even for the industry. In order for the model to take the right path, eccentric marketing principles must be applied. Then, I can assure you that your brand can work hard for you.

How do I determine my pricing strategy?

Pricing is one of the major factors of perception, but is not crucial to eccentric marketing. It plays a role in the overall decision of the consumer, however, so you have to consider the weight of price. Your total brand's deliverables, if they resonate with your target audience, may override the price factor. The total brand concept may move toward total emotional perfection for the consumer, especially if the consumer perceives an overwhelming emotional energy from the brand.

Given this, the brand must be priced according to the target audience. You should not exaggerate claims of quality, as so many in our culture do. Consumers will not perceive your product as "quality" unless it has been endorsed by friends and family, or even at times by the media. Many price their brands believing that the price reflects the quality. But there is a pricing factor that's also in place—the cost of producing the product versus the cost needed to make a profit. These are the basics. At times, eccentric price is a factor, but not as much as the other elements I have already discussed. So, while pricing does play a role, extremely over-priced brands can decline in market penetration because consumers may begin assessing their spending or may feel your brand is not "worth" the additional cost. You should not take your consumers' intelligence lightly. Speak to them through your total brand profile—many factors will make consumers believe that the journey to purchase your brand.

Imagine if you claimed that the ingredients of your product are of extremely high quality, yet the total brand profile has no clear identity. So, you set a high price for your product. In this case it is not likely your consumer will take the next step toward purchasing your brand—the first impact, the perception, does not exist without a clear identity in place. Second, the total emotional attributes are not in place either. Third, by this time, the customer has made his decision to walk away. So, what do you do now? You have definitely doomed the brand to the graveyard. So, when we talk about pricing, remember this: If you are asking more than your competitors, your brand must be have a clear identity and fulfill its promises. Those promises are called deliverables—you want to blind your audience to the high price by creating an overriding brand identity that will drive the consumer to purchase.

Some might consider my statements above and think, "What on earth is he talking about!?" But what I say is true. Think of it this way—why do consultants charge such high fees? It's because their *deliverables* are clear in their results and that's what their clients expect and need. During the initial phase, the client might decide to fire his consultant because he perceives (perhaps rightly so) that the consultant is not delivering. The firing can be fast.

The process is just the opposite when you work with a product, however. If the love union between the consumer and the brand is established, then it is hard for the consumer to let go unless something about the brand has gone awry. The price in this process is never the question—the energy of the brand and its emotional attributes are the real decision drivers, not the price. Therefore, in order for the eccentric marketing model to work, it has to be strictly business-to-consumer and not business-to-business. When we buy a brand we usually consider whether it is affordable or not, but at times we override that decision. That overriding factor lies in whether or not the brand is delivering and fulfilling the needs—and that results from its brand profile.

How important is marketing research?

I will speak firmly here about the state of market research on consumers. When the research contains enormous amounts of data, much of it is redundant and wasteful and few companies use the research to full advantage. I have little faith in full data research that claim error rates are about 5%. Consumers change their minds almost every day! For example, how have behavior patterns changed from the time you purchased the data?

On the other hand, many companies today avoid marketing research altogether, using minimal data to get a kick start. In the absence of what can be overwhelming research, they assume that as the consumer experiences the brand, the company will build the brand's adaptability to create consistency.

Of course, simple data about consumers from marketing research is very helpful to identify your consumer's age, lifestyle, location of work and residence and leisure habits. But the true answer for research lies, in my opinion, in the real experience the consumer has with the brand and whether the firm is capable of overseeing the behavior pattern of their consumers.

These models of marketing research must change the way facts are uncovered because marketing applications are not the same today as they were in the past. How brands worked 30 years ago is quite different from how brands work today. Within each sector of the industry, few brands today had the enormous and competitive base we see in today's consumer society. That's why the branding lifecycle has completely changed from previous eras. And, the life cycle will change even further as we face globalization and major mergers.

This is reality. Ask your office workers or employees at a retail store what the consumers are looking for. They will give you comprehensive insight—more so than a research firm will. Consumers' daily engagement with your company can help you compile a realistic supply of information to identify consumers' needs. Consumers will also provide you with firsthand information regarding their need and likes.

This is the element I strongly suggest for market research. You must understand the total physiological needs of your consumer. Here is where you will find true facts and emotions. With this information you can discover ways to establish the need and transform the brand into tangible products.

In addition, conduct market research with community leaders who influence society. Find them, talk to them about your brand so that they will talk about it to their friends, family and employees. This word-of-mouth endorsement can be most effective for your brand. Society's leaders endorsing your product through verbal communication can lift your brand further above your expectations and move it a step further into people's lives. So, while I believe in research, the most profound types of research I have explored are described above. This approach has brought results for me in many of the projects I have executed.

How important is need?

If you fulfill a need, you have definitely found a way to sell your brand. We all have needs, but each need differs from others, and various products will fulfill different needs. When you think of an idea, therefore, you must first establish what need it fulfills and then identify which segment of the market has this need.

Identifying and fulfilling a need is not an easy process; it's actually quite difficult. You must observe and identify the consumer's behavior and decide whether this need is a necessity or is secondary to necessity. This process is extremely vital to building a brand, because from there you establish the proper need and build on it.

For example, is "home delivery" a need? Yes it is. First, it becomes a need for customers who prefer the comfort of receiving goods in their own home, enjoy the convenience or if they don't have a means of transportation. So for this segment of customers, it is a need that can be fulfilled. Second, when an idea is based on reaching the consumer rather than on the consumer reaching the brands, the impact can be extremely effective. I truly believe the best way to achieve a proper end result is with ideas that reach consumers, because you're creating total need fulfillment. Consumers often prefer to be served rather than being asked to take the initiative.

CASE STUDY 2: Fork 'N Knife
Call. Order. EAT!

Feeling hungry, but your driver's gone on strike or maybe you've had a hectic day and heading to the kitchen is the last thing on your mind? Then look no further. Logic Holdings has the answer.

Logic Holdings—the brainchild of Marketing Strategist Said Aghil Baaghil—has developed a virtual restaurant with a kitchen-to-home concept called Fork-n-Knife, which allows customers to call a call center and place orders from a menu that includes a wide variety of foods such as breakfast omelets, toasts, sushi, salads, pastas, sandwiches, desserts and grilled seafood.

The dishes are prepared Western-style and served in large portions with minimum orders starting at SR25 for breakfast. Home delivery service is free of charge to any destination in the city with customers receiving their orders in less than 45 minutes.

The call center, located in the Al-Rawda district of Jeddah, has agents standing by 24 hours a day and seven days a week to assist customers with their orders. Beginning operations just last month, Fork—n-Knife, Baaghil said, has proven to be a very successful venture for the marketing company.

"The response we've received from customers on establishing Fork-n-Knife has been very positive because of the diverse menu we offer ranging from an array of dishes for breakfast, lunch, or dinner," Baaghil told Arab News.

"To improve the quality of service for our customers, we have recently leased a new kitchen that can handle staff of up to 120 workers and have hired an additional 45 professional chefs," said Baaghil.

"We employ our chefs according to the terms of a 90-day probation period in addition to training that we provide locally with the goal of making sure that they are truly professionals, able to handle the workload and able to provide our customers with the best quality dining experience there is to offer," he added.

When asked by Arab News what prompted him to create Fork-n-Knife, Baaghil said: "Because, I see the difference that we at Logic are making in the lives of people. My goal is to brand new ideas that were previously non-existent rather than creating something already known," he said.

Fork-n-Knife accepts order of all sizes from individual orders up to large-scale banquets, parties etc. For further details contact the call center at 02-6694348

—From *Arab News*

Here are other ways to think of needs: Is knowledge a need? Definitely. It's a need, but can it be fulfilled? Yes, if one is determined to obtain that knowledge. Therefore, is online education a need? Yes, it is a need because many cannot attend a university in person because of work or other factors such as location or time constraints. Consumers would like to fulfill their need for knowledge, and that's why online education is booming. Is publishing-on-demand a need? Yes it is, because there are many authors who might otherwise be denied a chance to express their opinions or share their stories by traditional publishers. Instead, companies like iUniverse are fulfilling the need for self-publishing or publishing-on-demand.

A need is a fruitful aspect of marketing when addressing consumers. Wherever there is need, there is always a fruitful future for a brand. Therefore, don't take needs lightly; bank on them for the future of your brand. I based eccentric marketing on need and fulfillment. Emotions constitute need; any sense of human satisfaction is a strong need. Reach it, and you will establish a brand.

How important is color to a brand?

Colors are essential in the process of building your brand. You must identify what each color stands for and how it communicates to the audience. The other factor of colors is the classification. This depends on what level of society you're targeting as far as culture, income, and upbringing.

For example, when you think of red, it has a vibrant energy; its colors are mainly used in food products. Green is for health, white connotes purity, black represents class and prestige, navy blue indicates a corporate high-end business world, baby blue is used for newborns and usually works well with younger audiences, pink represents a strong youthful femininity and orange is a color of festivity that usually works well for brands that represents the seaside.

When you think of the upper end of society, you can do well in using all dark colors, such as black, fire red, dark green and dark oak. When you think of middle-class, you will go with a variety of colors; you will find red useful as a moving color, with orange, green and purple for the lighter side. How we use colors on brands is a very important aspect of the product. Each color will resonate differently with the audience to whom you're addressing the brand.

You cannot mix and match or take this issue lightly if your knowledge of the world of branding is weak. Colors play a big part in perception and emotions, and colors can also create the brand's general environment. That's why if you are building a brand, consult professionals who can assist you with this issue. Don't have your CEO or the business owner tamper with it unless he has adequate background knowledge.

How do I name my brands?

When you name a brand, keep it simple. You want it to be easily understood by your audience, so don't give it a name that is far from what the brand represents. Your audience will be lost completely. How you name it will depend upon which audience you're addressing, both age-wise and socially. This is a critical issue! If the name is not appropriate you will have a problem.

In the Middle East region, some love to put their family names on products. While this is generally acceptable, if you can create a better name than the family name, then do so! The name will help you sell your brand. For example, if you named a health food restaurant "Quick Fit," will the name sell? Probably not, because the name leads the mind to believe that the product is associated with a car maintenance garage. On the other hand, if you have a store that sells diet products and you name it "The Diet Shop," the name says it all. It is easy for consumers to associate the second name more quickly than the first. It's very simple. Don't complicate the name; make it so that it won't be hard for your audience to observe what the name stands for.

For example, a rental car company decided to name its brand "Modern." The question with this name is: What does the name have to do with a rental car company? Really, the answer is "none," so the chances of this rental car company reaching its target audience are not good. On the other hand I once had a client who asked me to create a name for a rental car company. I decided to simplify it so the name will say it all. I came up with the name Rent & Drive. In this case the name says what the company is all about. Some like to complicate the name issue; you find many companies in our market who name their brands to imply much more than what the brand is really about. The name should sum up the whole concept of what the brand is and for what purpose. The accompanying case study, on APEX Limo service provides a good example of a brand name that's right on target with the audience it wishes to serve.

CASE STUDY 3: APEX: Luxury Chauffeur Service

What is APEX?

The first luxury limo service in Jeddah for business and leisure specializing in airport transfers and conference transportation.

Treat yourself.

APEX, a luxury chauffeur service company, was recently launched under the management of LOGIC, a leading marketing firm responsible for the success of various companies that are now making names in the Jeddah business community.

With *"Treat Yourself"* as their slogan, APEX provides unparalleled chauffeur service to customers for their ground transportation needs using the finest vehicles equipped with refreshments and electronic gadgets such as DVD with LCD, Laptop and Mobile phone to assist travelers. With courteous, experienced and professionally attired chauffeurs, APEX aims to provide a high level of service to their customers.

Their services are available within Jeddah throughout Makkah and Madinah. Customers may use APEX for airport pick up and drop off, business transport service, city tours (dining and shopping), religious trips, Obhur beach trip, full day service and other personal needs. APEX charges for as low as SAR 80 per hour for their services.

Most recently, APEX launched a Tourism Program called "Discover Jeddah". Featuring different packages to explore and enjoy the city with the APEX Chauffeur as tourist guide.

The tourism program was launched with a mission to acquaint tourists and locals with the city and present Jeddah's richness in culture and traditions. APEX was the first in the industry to introduce and promote Jeddah as a tourist destination.

Service bookings are done through APEX' own call center (02 284 2626) where they have customer service agents available 24 hours a day. However, APEX accepts online bookings and reservations done through their website (www.apexsaudi.com). Customers are given 15% off the total service charge when they book online.

How important is market segmentation?

Prior to developing any marketing strategy, you must define market segmentation. You must define your audience by *segmenting* from the general audience a subgroup of people whose attitudes and behaviors will match the marketing strategy you have in mind for your product. Once you have determined that these subgroups have similar needs and likes, you have identified the audience for whom you will build your brand.

Market segmentation involves a wide range of audience dissection down to the particular subgroup. It is an extremely essential process for brand success. You must consider whether this subgroup of people is growing; as a certain percentage of the population will grow from year to year. One main concern to consider in developing your strategy is how well the brand and the brand managers are equipped to maintain consistency within the brand as it is perceived by the audience in the initial stage. Also, remember that your subgroup will age and the brand may face generational decline if it does not keep innovating to address the newcomers to your target audience. Basically, brands must change with general cultural trends in order to stay relevant to your audience.

My key example for this would be a confectionary company that has been around 30 years in the Saudi Arabian market. During the initial phase of its brand's lifecycle, it identified the subgroup audience to whom they would address the brand. Soon, the brand started to face an enormous decline. This is because the owners of the brand failed to address the new incoming generation. What I liked 30 years ago at the age of fifteen is different from today at age 45. I am less interested in buying confectionaries from a store, but my son is interested. The brand, however, is not appealing to my son because the total brand image was not modified to account for new trends among the owner's initially-identified target audience. This is a critical situation when considering a subgroup from the market as a segment. You might communicate to them, but when the brand can't attract the "newcomers" to your segment, consider it dead.

Advertising: Is It Worth It?

Advertising is the core avenue for communicating about your brand; without communication the brand will be stagnant. Adverting, therefore, is essential. Keep in mind, however, that based on your market segmentation, each subgroup represents only a certain percent of the total population. For example, a subgroup could be only 7% of the total population. In this case, communication such as advertising could be very expensive. For such special subgroups ("market niches"), word-of-mouth and endorsements from social leaders are more effective. Public relations—if it involves press endorsements—community events and other methods will be more effective in bringing a "niche" brand to life than advertising.

Furthermore, advertising today plays the role of making claims that can't necessarily be verified. Consumers don't have as much faith or belief in advertising as they do in the claims of friends, family, co-workers, community leaders and public figures. Word-of-mouth and endorsements have worked very well, as many of the brands that take this approach are very effective today. Once a brand has launched, it needs endorsements based on consumer's experiences. Other advertising methods are not regarded as proper endorsements, but rather as the brand making its own claims. Once the brand is well-endorsed from the public relations platform and has its place in the market, advertising can play a key role in reminding the consumer that your brand exists.

In fact, the way advertising has been conducted in our region has driven many consumers away from brands. That's because of false claims, such as the overuse of that word "quality" as discussed earlier. Such a claim has made the worth of the advertising campaign minimal. Think about it—if you have a brand that is finding its way, what would you prefer to do? Advertise it everywhere, with minimal effect? (Remember, the costs of advertising are horrendous in this part of the world.) Or, would you prefer to have your brand be engaged personally through consumer experience, events and other public relations platforms? Event sponsorship, for example, is effective for the brand because it becomes available on location; the public can gain immediate experience with your products.

When we think of advertising today, there are certainly many advertising agencies. But again, there are many elements you will have to consider to gain the true worth of these advertising agencies. Elements include their professional profile as well as which brands they have served and whether those brands have flourished. It is a sad reality in our regional market to see how easily one can obtain a license to open an advertising agency, how much these less proficient agencies affect the industry and agencies that are well-qualified. Think about what I just said: If I'm not convincing, go ahead and try any agency that suits your fancy. But once your brand fails, avoid bringing on a marketing consultant—because brands are like humans. They live and die and the cure for any of their problems is far more expensive and far more difficult than you realize. My advice is this: think about it before you do it, and think about what you would like your brand to be in the long term.

SIDEBAR 2: Client-Agency Relations

Client-agency relations are one of the most problematic issues in the life cycle of a brand in Saudi Arabia.

Specialized local and multi-national ad agencies prefer to handle multi-national accounts or well planned local companies' accounts. Because of the properly structured marketing departments within those organizations, their briefs are detailed and they assist the agency in the overall communication strategy.

On the other hand, many local firms in Saudi Arabia fail to set up a proper marketing department due to the misconceptions between marketing and sales. In addition, when introducing a brand, a local ad agency appeals to them because they will face less paperwork, a less-structured system and be more familiar with culture and traditions than with a fully fledged international ad agency.

In my opinion, the decision should be based on how experienced the agency is in delivering the communication related to the brand rather than being categorized by nationality.

Clients are confused as to what communication tools to use; some agencies not only provide BTL or ATL but they intend to stretch the communication budget of the client as a sales point and do not estimate that a professional marketing department needs to assess all CPM (cost per impression) spending as it relates to their target audience.

Who is to blame? The basic problem is having the proper knowledge of what an advertising agency's scope of work entails and understanding the role of a structured, efficient marketing department.

Over the past 20 years, the role of a marketing department within a local company has grown, along with its duty.

Today, 30% of the companies in the market that are local firms have a proper marketing department that functions to serve its target audience. On the other hand, the city of Jeddah has 4,500 small-scale and larger-scale advertising agencies, both local and international, with the local ad agencies comprising 95% of the market. Are they all qualified as advocates of proper branding and communications?

I would say not, only few. But this has caused a misrepresentation of the word advertising in the Kingdom and the industry, as the difference between a media house and an ad agency has not been classified properly. The potential is enormous for many of the local firms if they seek to acquire total brand mechanisms, and as you all know, brands are a part of human nature.

The potential of developing the client-agency relationship is also enormous considering the basic principles from parties. An agency expects a detailed and proper briefing of the brand and its direction, which is basically produced by the marketing department of the client. Secondly, clients must observe the best form of communication strategy in order to reach the desired end results. Ad agencies constantly find clients' knowledge of brand direction very vague, and changing direction causes the agency to fail in parts of their communication.

Clients on the other hand, have a difficult time finding a reputable, proper advertising agency that will serve their needs. Multi-national ad agencies prefer to classify their client types to create a highly esteemed portfolio for their firm. Many local firms also outsource from neighbouring countries such as Egypt and Jordan because of the price factor.

I truly believe that the awareness of the importance of having properly structured local ad agencies is on the way since many clients are seeking professionalism and experience within the field to assist them in delivering their brand objectives.

Agency and client 2007 Gulf Marketing Review

Do brand line extensions work?

I think of brand line extension like this: When my parents got married and decided to have children, what would the result be if they named all four children by variations on a single name? What if they named the first Said, the second Said Light, the third Said Extreme and the fourth Said Fusion? My other family members and family friends will only relate to me Said, and not all the extended Saids. Branding is the same as naming children: each brand has to have an individual identity and personality. It is true brand extensions will receive some consumer engagement, but they won't be as effective as the first brand you launch.

When you think of brands you have to apply the same principles as naming your children. Each brand has its own life and shouldn't be burdened with seven other lives. It has the right to live and do what it is known for. In my opinion, the extension brand is nothing but a simple market engagement with minimal effect on market share percentage. In the long run the risk for the extended brand to decline is very high.

Let me give you a number of examples. First, can a milk brand known from the beginning as a "milk brand" in later years become a "juice brand?" As a consumer your first impression and union with the brand perception, decision and emotion was the milk brand. If the brand changes to fresh juice, it will be harder to observe and understand because your mind is set as milk, not juice. Another example is Ice Cube, the famous rapper. Your perception of him is probably that he is a great rapper. Imagine, however, if he introduced himself tomorrow as the heavy metal musician, going so far as to produce a heavy metal album. The chance Ice Cube's heavy metal album will flop is very high, because the consumer's initial experience is with Ice Cube as a rapper. Not only will his sales likely decline, but he has also damaged his total brand equity. Finally, think about Sony. We all know Sony as the digital king in its category. What if Sony decided to introduce their high-end digital sounds in a Sony restaurant? Would it work?

In sum, why extend a brand if your brand is known for on thing; it shouldn't be thought of in many other ways. Your audience will remember the first experience they have with your brand. Let's put it this way: brands are only identified as one in thing in the eye of the beholder and not for many things.

Some corporations prefer to build brand line extensions to capitalize on the assets of the initial brand in terms of stock value. But the long-term result of that extended brand is almost non-existent. The gradual growth of a brand gives it a better chance to live and flourish globally. Focusing on the initial brand will help it attain maximum growth, rather than extending it to many different lines of products.

Market segmentation plays a role with brand extensions as well. Imagine I have a carbonated drink called XYZ and it's full of sugar.

Then let's say that later I decide to introduce a zero sugar drink to a new subgroup that is diet- and health-oriented. Which is better—to name it XYZ, just like the one that the whole world knows is full of sugar? Or would it be better to create a new name, personality and product profile that has emotional attributes and fulfills a need, thus engaging the new subgroup? If your choice is still to name your new product after your initial product, remember that some have done it, but the results have not been happy ones. When you build individuality into brands, they create their own center of attention. Brands can maneuver within the market as they wish, even if that brand is not the first of its kind, but a brother to another brand.

Do all marketing applications apply?

Marketing basics, or the principles of marketing, apply to any new model of marketing, including eccentric marketing. Eccentric marketing is an added value to a brand, from inception as a concept to the final phase of launching and selling the brand. It includes the total marketing strategy that is needed to penetrate the target audience. Modifying marketing from its roots is like changing the basic foundation that has worked for many brands. Eccentric marketing works on market segmentation and the essential need to create a market segment for your brand. No matter how large a percentage of the total population is considered, the idea is to identify and build a brand that will satisfy the need of your identified target market.

Without the general principles of marketing, eccentric marketing cannot work. It is essential to use all marketing applications when you try to reach consumers. Having the added values of creativity and innovation—characteristic of eccentric marketing—will differentiate you from the rest of the brands. How you market your product and how you plan to deploy your strategies are important aspects as well. That's why when you think of marketing applications, you must consider more than what will push the brand forward and help it live longer than its competitors.

The true nature of marketing is that it's the heart of any organization that plans to be engaged in business activities with consumers or other businesses. Without marketing, the company will be doomed. If it weren't so tragic, it would be comical how many companies in our region, both large and small, neglect the importance of marketing. We witness the truth of this in that our brands. Despite all our resources and financial capabilities, we are not able to expand outside of our region. Some do, and others are catching up at a very slow pace. For all the claims of numerous activities of our brands around the globe, our market still operates mainly through small businesses. We have more retailers and privately-owned businesses than any other place in the world. Think about this: Where are we going to be without marketing in the next ten years? I will let you answer that.

Do I have the "right" combination of the elements?

Once we combine perception with emotions and decisions, then we have brought together the mix necessary for the brand to be live, be active and to penetrate the target audience. But the question remains: How *great* is the need for this brand you have created? Is it an extreme need, moderate need or just a need? Once you have identified that level, then you can start building on the total combination of brand elements needed to sell the product.

It all starts with an idea. The idea must be composed of ways to generate revenue and be developed properly into a business model. From there, creating the brand's profile takes place. That includes the name, the emotional attributes, the brand personality—the total equity, or value, of the brand. It should be as real and tangible as possible, to communicate with and be observed by humans and in particular the target audience with the correct demographic and psychographic characteristics. The consumer's perception makes an impact on the consumer's attraction to the product. With a positive first impression, feelings generated, along with emotional impact, and this is what creates a complete attribute for your audience. For example if you are about to launch a high-end brand, the first thing you must consider is the target audience. Define the age, the social class and spend time studying their likes and observe their emotional desires. Then if say your demographic is between 20–30 years old and in an upper social class, the use of things such as color and font type on your brand identity must be used properly according to their likes. For this group, the use of color would be mainly alpha colors such as black, navy blue, fire red, dark olive green, purple and blues. All these states create perception because colors do create an environment for the eye. The environment and design of the profile and the color used are the actual starting point of perception.

The decision is then made to buy and make this brand a part of the consumer's life like every other element that exists—such as your car and even your wife or husband. The total combination of the elements is workable if the audience is defined prior to developing the brand. This includes even the name of the brand.

Once the combinations are built, then segmenting your audience and implementing a total marketing strategy can bring the brand to life. The deeper part of building a brand evolves through deeper thought and creativity because you are linking your product to the likes of the target audience. Such a process requires many elements be united and that you attach many parts together. The emotion of a brand is the union with the consumer. Once the brand is living in unity with its audience, the brand fulfils the emotional attribute, and the union will last. If the brands begins to detour or differ from its original impression, then the union starts to break down.

Aligning all elements is not an easy process, but you must align them to meet the desires of your audience and not your own personal needs. You must consider what your brand is about so that you can create something that will live with and communicate to the audience, something that will be shared and have a natural course of life. Once the audience grows apart from the brand, the brand must be renovated for incoming generations; it flows with the continuance of generations.

I emphasis these elements is because once you have established the generic marketing mix, there must be more value added to your product with creativity and innovation in order to achieve the impact of perception, decision and sentiment. The power of the brand is not on selling, but how close to human needs the brand is in order to penetrate the lives of the audience.

Chapter 6

THINK GLOBALLY, ACT GLOBALLY

What about Globalization?

In this era of globalization, major European, American and Asian firms are penetrating brands all over the world and in our own neighborhoods. Yet we don't yet have the competitive edge to compete locally or even globally. Big organizations from abroad are implementing merger and acquisition strategies to expand their consumer base. Local firms appreciate these mergers because those brands are foreign owned, have a proper global branding strategy, and are cash generators. Our local brands still fail to meet customer expectations and confidence, however. We must act *today* to brand our products, deployed with marketing applications, so that in the long term we have a global competitive edge.

This change in our region must be taken seriously.

To this point, I have addressed all Arab business owners, small and large scale firms alike, regarding the essential function of marketing in their companies. I have also stressed the importance of branding, and if the marketing department excels in its duties, any business can be profitable. Basically, without marketing consider your firm doomed.

As I've repeatedly stated, most owners have given themselves the prestigious title of CEO without understanding the core of the job description and the duties it follows. This statement is meant specifically for CEO who at times is also the business owner. He should be aware of the potential of the marketing world and how branding can attain results. In this chapter, I would like to address those who don't have an in-depth understanding of marketing, but may have learned something from this book up to this point.

First, I urge you to take chances and enlighten yourselves about marketing concepts. This is for the sake of our brands, so that they can compete globally. I am taking the initiative to push this need and I will continue to push until something happens that will support the advancement of our brands.

Second, I believe most CEOs are responsible for the fact that our brands are not expanding in market appeal beyond our region. After all, CEOs are fully responsible for every decision regarding the brands' geographical mobility. CEOs need to realize that Arabs are not the only consumers who appreciate our brands! There are potential new customers all over the world; the target audiences exist and you need only deploy proper strategies to reach them. The world, as we have heard constantly, is becoming a macro-market. To ensure our brands are not lost in the global market, we need to set short- and long-term strategies to move ahead. Be confident about your brand and let's move it forward.

Third, I totally understand there are many elements involved in market expansion. But if the proper planning does not start today, when will it start? Our consumers are wooed by foreign brands from across the globe; their confidence in imported brands is much stronger due to the effects of both brand presentation and global strategy. We must realize that if we don't initiate our moves today, we don't know when we will see a difference. The reason I address the CEO community about the importance of moving forward is because most CEOs are business owners here in our region. They, not the teams behind them, are fully responsible for the life cycle of their brands. They decide on every move of the brand. It is a pity that at times a CEO may take it personally and disagree with his or her team based on personal reasons rather than on the total equity of his business. Such unprofessional behavior can never help us push our brands to their ultimate potential in this era of globalization.

Fourth, I am arguing this case for the best interests of our region. We have the chance to see how to work with models and move away from being 100% interested in working just with brand agents of our own region. We can initiate a new goal: to search for agents who can represent our brands in their countries or across the globe. I might sound angry here. I am, in a way, because I can do nothing as an individual. I need every private sector business owner to invest a certain concern for his brand for the good of our region. I understand how important it is for global brands to exist in our region and I am all for that—but equal trade is better for the global market's needs, and for the benefit of our region as providers and not just as consumers.

Fifth, global consumers may desire our brands, but our initiative is very weak right now; it needs to move forward. Let's again consider the companies of the Asia-Pacific region. Observe how they function as global competitors. The least we can say is that their brands exist in the Western market and are competing viably with local counterparts. My desire for our brands should thus be clear. We should set forward all possible resources to assist in achieving our goals.

Our Young CEOs

The future looks bright for incoming generations of CEOs—the young who are launching their own start-up companies or who took over their family business and are working to shape it. Some of these young incoming CEOs face the trouble, however, that they are just following what their fore fathers practiced, fearing that change will cause an enormous decline for what has been built. The fact is that these young CEOs are active for change, can see that change will bring globalization for a stagnant market, have a voice for their brands and can sense that brands will attain proper cash flow. These young CEOs in our region are also setting up properly structured firms, while the old-school CEOs resist making any changes. They resist change even though their direct consumers' needs are changing through the generations.

The fact is this: these young incoming CEOs are highly motivated and are speaking today's business language. If these next-generation entrepreneurs can learn what today's business world holds in terms of proper financial departments and marketing, they one day our region will hold strong stakes in the global economy. I strongly count on these young entrepreneurs to make a difference and ensure our brands flourish around the globe. Young CEOs are the hope of tomorrow for our brands to flourish in the global market, but they must be heard and do what's good for the region, The call for action can only be executed by the incoming generations of CEO's while the old school CEO'S must rest and allow the generation change at this time of the world of globalization.

Those few who are not aware and blindly follow the old system, inherited through generations, will see their companies downsize from five thousand employees to one hundred employees—due to the fact that change was not accounted for.

Today we also see young regional CEOs promising to change how we conduct our marketing efforts. These select members of the future generation are mostly involved in start-up operations of mid-size companies. Others are blending into the massive operations run by their fathers and forefathers.

When you think of the market a century ago, there were few companies operating in each industry. But now, these few have grown tremendously. Today each industry is experiencing local and multi-national competition. And it will all come down to a war of brands. Those brands that are owned by well-structured, progressively operated companies will be likely to dominate their category of industry. There will be a few small-scale firms who have the chance to gain market share, even if they are properly structured in terms of organization.

The sad part is that older-generation business people—a few, if not all of them—don't see these factors. Perhaps they intend to ignore the new reality and go with their assumptions. What if you hired a reputable financial institution and asked how much risk you would have if your business decisions were based only on assumptions? What they will tell you will not make you happy. Business decisions—financial or marketing—cannot be made on assumptions. I will say this: let the professionals in each field assist you in fulfilling your needs. At the end of the day, this move will attain satisfactory results for your firm. We must move away from assumptions when thinking about marketing, because marketing is reality.

With this said, let us ask: How important is it to be aware about marketing and its purpose? I think it's extremely important. Think about companies requesting literature about what to do with their marketing department. This is a perfect situation for the regional marketing association. Its role would be to assist companies with all of their marketing inquiries. A regional marketing association would work hard to provide global market information to assist those who intend to penetrate new markets outside of our region. Many companies are missing the proper guidelines; with an active marketing association, we will witness a significant difference in how brands are marketed and where we will be ten years from now.

Today many marketers can lead our brands outside of the region. The time has come for marketers in the Middle East to dedicate themselves to transforming our products into well-recognized multinational brands. Yet something is holding us back. The truth is that local firms lack a basic understanding of what marketing truly is and, as a result, ignore its importance as core element of the business model.

The problems start at university level. Most of the universities in the region do not offer marketing as a core major, but only as an extension of other majors. Then, there is a lack of knowledge of what marketing actually is. The translation of marketing in Arabic is Al Tasweeq, which basically means: "the act of selling products in the markets." This has further confused the validity of what marketing is and its variety of applications.

A Call to Action

My biggest concern is whether I will ever see a day where the art of marketing, with all its nuances, is implemented to full effect in our region. Will I ever see any of our home-grown FMCGs flourishing on a global scale rather than just the local markets? I am a passionate marketing advocate whose goal is to see any one of our consumer brands on supermarket shelves around the globe. But this will never happen unless those in the local market accept the responsibility of educating themselves on the basic principles of marketing.

While the concept of brand positioning was created by Al Rise and Jack Trout some 20 years ago, it has only reached our region comparatively recently, and many marketers and ad agencies have yet to adopt the full principles of positioning.

This proves just how far behind we are in adapting and transforming. This is dangerous when we consider how far off we are, especially in this era of globalization, when many brands are perfectly synchronized within one point or place through things such as eCommerce.

Will the next generation of young marketers face these changes proactively, and recognize the potential financial rewards that follow? Here is my succinct call to action:

First, we must establish a regional marketing association that will assist brand owners in fulfilling their potential. This association would also refer them to professionals who can assist with brand building and find models that will benefit them within a larger spectrum.

We must start from home base in all industries and initiate an oversight panel. Let's work together to enable our market to flourish. I am asking for everyone's involvement—from all countries in our region—in order to set up this association that will help us penetrate all possibilities for our brands.

We are a well-equipped society with an enormous potential, and deploying an association might be hard at first. But there is always a starting point, and perhaps that start will come from this book. We have the manpower, the financials and the institutions to succeed.

We are better off then a lot of regions, but what we are missing is the initiative and the guidelines.

Second, I sincerely suggest that we first redefine the meaning of "marketing" in Arabic and move away from the word "Tasweeq," since its ambiguity does not help in its effectiveness. Tasweeq, merely implies shopping, sales and getting products off the shelves. Redefining the meaning is the first step in the right direction.

Third, we should add the marketing a major in the university syllabus as an alternative to general business administration majors.

Fourth, we should encourage community involvement and create public awareness of what marketing is, its purpose, and value.

Fifth, and finally it will take every firm, every marketer and every organization to move forward as a team so that one day we, the Arabs, have our brands visible in the lives of all global consumers on a par with competitive foreign multinationals.

If we can pull together and manage all this, then we will see growth and a complete change in how we think of marketing and what it is, and its crucial role in our organizations.

CONCLUSION

In this book, I have examined the current state of business industries in the thriving Arab world. I urge owners of small and large businesses to rethink the role of the CEO in branding and marketing. I have examined the prevalent issues that I claim are holding back Arab companies from truly going global: personal ego, cultural habits and not understanding what marketing is really about.

The book goes on to examine the basic principles and decisions needed to create a successful brand. I have identified current common mistakes throughout the process and explained what I believe are solutions to these mistakes.

Eccentric marketing is the core of my work and I have explained the concept of eccentric marketing here as a specific strategy for reaching specific target audiences in today's increasingly connected world. I have achieved successful branding using eccentric marketing concepts (see After Word). With the current problems in our region, eccentric marketing is the solution to attain results. You have seen some of these results in the case studies I've presented. Each has been a successful brand in the Kingdom of Saudi Arabia, targeting audiences age 18 and over. I hope you've noticed how these models differentiated various concepts because of an identified need for the demographic to experience products or services in keeping with their behavior and lifestyle.

Most of all, I have put my own principles into practice with the successful launch of LOGIC (see After Word). Anyone living in the city of Jeddah will truly speak of their experience with LOGIC as either a consumer or even a competitor. By launching LOGIC, not only did I develop the eccentric marketing model, but with experience, I have improved the efficiency of the model. The success of various services and establishments in Saudi Arabia serve as tangible testimonials to the sound principles behind eccentric marketing. If CEOs and business owners are concerned with proper marketing for our region, they can reach out and grasp the concepts using eccentric marketing.

In closing, my highest hope is a call for change. We must embrace change and give marketing due process so that our brands can prosper in the global market and be competitive. The best place to start this change is from the office of the business owner or CEO. With this book, that change can begin to gather momentum.

AFTERWORD:
LOGIC MARKETING

In 2004, I established a company named LOGIC for a Saudi business owner. It is an eccentric marketing company specializing in the food and leisure industries. These are industries that have shown significant growth in recent years and are expected to continue to do so in the coming years.

Since its launch, LOGIC has been a consistent pioneer and is well-known for introducing unique concepts and services to the market. Hence, LOGIC's image and reputation has evolved into a business "trendsetter."

Through LOGIC, I have worked to create brands that fulfill a particular target group's needs. The brands are unique, innovative and dynamic in terms of their profile and brand personification. Today LOGIC has taken the city of Jeddah in Saudi Arabia by storm, within the aforementioned industries. Within a year and half, we have created ten different brands and create the most amazing concepts based on consumer needs. We have focused on three categories: retail dining, restaurants reaching the home market and luxury passenger transportation. These were identified as special needs for the city, especially within the demographic of upper-class society.

When I was first asked by the chairman of the group to come to Saudi Arabia, I thought about spending a few months just to study the particular needs of the city of Jeddah. What were its consumer habits? What were its demographics? The outcome of my research was loud and clear: a huge demand existed within the city for the luxury lifestyle. The city is largely populated by people between the ages of 16 to 40 with both time and money on their hands.

The city's primary entertainment activities are supermarket shopping, clothes shopping and dining out. The demographic feels cluttered within the existing restaurant environment. What could LOGIC do for that demographic? The answer was to build a company that would introduce eccentric brands to the area.

Our first brand was Pearls Café, an eatery that would provide an alternative environment to what currently exists in the city. On November 23, 2005, the first LOGIC brand, therefore, was born. The café was a huge success and everyone in the target demographic made plans to visit it. The brand concept was built to satisfy a need of the city's demographic. If you live in the Jeddah, Kingdom of Saudi Arabia, you've had to have heard of Pearls.

The second brand to follow was also in the restaurant retail category. Here came what I must say was one of my crowning achievements. For the theme restaurant Black Rose, I worked on every thought and idea even more so than I did with Pearls. I wanted to create the first "theme" restaurant in the city of Jeddah. Everything at the Black Rose lounge is very aligned, from the door to the interior. It is one of the city's top spots for fine dining.

My next project went in a very different direction, to the world of health. I introduced Eater, a fast-food concept in which the food offered is free of preservatives. Today, Eater has grown to meet the niche demand of the health-conscious residents in the city. Another new venture is Yalla Utlob, a restaurant specializing in home delivery.

There are many restaurants in the city, but not all of them provide home delivery services. So we created Yalla Utlob to cater to that need. Yalla Utlob serves all of all restaurants in the city, including our own.

Next came Apex, a luxury chauffeur service. Apex provides the fine touch of the image of a chauffeur—well-attuned to service, with fine manners and proper gesturers. Apex serves key hotels in the city and provides personal service whenever needed. Recently Apex introduced a travel program for incoming tourists called "Discover Jeddah."

From here, I diversified my strategy to create a new concept of service that consists of three brands: Fork 'n Knife, for typical American dinners delivered straight to your home; Wonder Burger, and Sweet Box—a virtual pastry shop that also delivers straight to your home.

All these brands are meant to demonstrate that LOGIC—and eccentric marketing—have been making a mark in the city within its targeted audiences. The future of LOGIC is promising; we plan to expand to other cities. This decision, of course, depends on the owners of the businesses. As for me, I am finding that there is a high demand for LOGIC's services, and I fully anticipate that more innovative ideas will spring forth from the company.

As I'm sure you can tell, I am very proud of what I have done with the company and the brands created. I believe, however, that any firm in Saudi Arabia, or even in the region, can proceed to instant growth if two critical departments are very well-equipped with the right people and sufficient budgets: marketing and finance. These two departments are closely related to one another; their link is strong. In terms of assessing and planning, they are the heart of any business model and are needed to accomplish company goals and to flourish. They, more than most departments, have cold hard facts that they face daily regarding the health of your business.

I hope one day I will see LOGIC flourish further, whether I am still with the company or not. But LOGIC is definitely my best creation and it proved to me that my model of eccentric marketing has worked. I have seen it take hold of Jeddah, whose residents now think and live with its brands. The company and its brands are trend-setters and that's specifically how it is positioned in the market. Being a trendsetter is not an easy process—it means to lead a community and convince a city to become emotionally connected and to buy into what you have created. This is my prime example of how eccentric marketing works for specific target audiences.

978-0-595-46593-4
0-595-46593-5

www.ingramcontent.com/pod-product-compliance
Lightning Source LLC
Chambersburg PA
CBHW030850180526
45163CB00004B/1521